P9-CEG-917

A Tenderfoot Bride

PIKE'S PEAK FROM THE OLD RANCH

A Tenderfoot Bride

TALES FROM AN OLD RANCH

BY

Clarice E. Richards

Introduction by Maxine Benson

University of Nebraska Press
Lincoln and London

Copyright 1920 by the Fleming H. Revell Company
Renewel copyright © 1947 by Clarice E. Richards
Introduction copyright © 1988 by the University of Ne-
braska Press
All rights reserved
Manufactured in the United States of America

First Bison Book printing: 1988
Most recent printing indicated by the first digit below:
1   2   3   4   5   6   7   8   9   10

Library of Congress Cataloging-in-Publication Data
Richards, Clarice E.
    A tenderfoot bride: tales from an old ranch / by Clar-
ice E. Richards: introduction by Maxine Benson.
        p. cm.
    "Bison book."
    Reprint. Originally published: New York: F. H. Revell
Co., 1920.
    ISBN 0-8032-3889-4. ISBN 0-8032-8930-8 (pbk.)
    1. Richards, Clarice E. 2. Ranch life—Colorado—El-
bert County—History—20th century. 3. Pioneers—
Colorado—Elbert County—Biography. 4. Elbert County
(Colo.)—Social life and customs. 5. Women pioneers—
Colorado—Elbert County—Biography. I. Title.
F782.E25R53 1988
978.8'8703'0924—dc19   CIP 88-14347
[B]

Reprinted from the 1920 edition published by the Fleming H. Revell Company, New York

The University of Nebraska Press has made every effort
to trace the holder of the renewal copyright or her heir.
If he or she still exists, we ask the present copyright
holder to make himself or herself known and accept our
excuses for proceeding with the reprinting of this work.

978.887030 92
R514at
1988

To the One
whose Companionship, Inspiration and
Encouragement have made
this book possible
My Husband

CONTENTS

ILLUSTRATIONS

INTRODUCTION
by Maxine Benson

Clarice Richards came as a bride to a ranch on the high plains of Elbert County, Colorado. Before long she overcame her initial diffidence and resolved to meet head-on her responsibilities as mistress of a remote ranch. In the process she learned as much about herself as about ranching, as she later noted in *A Tenderfoot Bride*. Written with insight and humor, the book records one woman's coming of age as well as the passing of an era.

Born in Dayton, Ohio, in 1875, Clarice had come to the ranch as the bride of Jarvis Richards ("Owen Brook" in her book), born to an old New England family in Charlestown, New Hampshire, in 1852. An 1875 Dartmouth graduate, he had attended the Andover Theological Seminary and was ordained a Congregational minister following his graduation in 1878. After serving two churches in Vermont, he accepted a pastoral assignment in Spearfish, Dakota Territory, in 1881.[1]

Meanwhile, Jarvis's brother, Bartlett, ten years his junior, had gone to Wyoming in 1879. Shortly thereafter, Bartlett Richards began managing cattle ranches in Wyoming, and within a few years he commanded an empire covering vast stretches of eastern Wyoming and western Nebraska. His Spade Ranch in the Nebraska Sandhills (the brand was an ace of spades) was near Old Jules Sandoz's place, and the often adversarial relationship between cattle baron and settlers has been chronicled by Mari Sandoz in such works as *Old Jules* and *The Cattlemen*.[2]

By 1885 another Richards brother, DeForest, had also ventured west. Born in 1846, DeForest had moved to Alabama during Reconstruction when his father bought land in the central part of the state. Active in politics as county sheriff and treasurer, DeForest had pursued business interests in Camden, Alabama, before joining Bartlett. The two brothers started a bank at Chadron, Nebraska, in 1885, but within a few years DeForest had moved on to Wyoming where he founded the First National Bank of Douglas and served as mayor of the town. Elected governor of Wyoming in 1898, he died in 1903 shortly after beginning his second four-year term.[3]

While DeForest was establishing himself, Jarvis Richards left Spearfish in 1886 and spent two years traveling and studying in Europe at the universities of Berlin and Leipzig. He then joined Bartlett at the Spade Ranch, where in Mari Sandoz's words he was "general manager, purchasing agent, and all-around utility man in charge of everything from windmills and mowers to hiring wolfers to clear out the gray wolves that pulled down yearling heifers in winter snow." When the Nebraska Land and Feeding Company was formed in 1899, merging the vast assets of two earlier corporations (including the Spade), Jarvis was named secretary-treasurer; Bartlett headed the firm as president.[4]

As the Richards brothers were making their mark in ranching and politics, Clarice Estabrook came to Nebraska one summer during the late 1890s to visit her friend Inez Richards. Inez, born in 1873 while her father DeForest was still in Alabama, had married her Uncle Bartlett in 1897. Three years later, on May 24, 1900, Clarice and Jarvis were married in Dayton, and soon the newlyweds were traveling to the ranch that Jarvis had bought in Elbert County, Colorado. (Some idea of the interlocking nature of the Richards brothers' affairs can be gained by noting that one-half of the stock of the Bijou Ranch Company, which carried Jarvis's name as president, was apparently owned by the Nebraska Land and Feeding Company. Bartlett Richards's partner, Will Comstock, was vice-president of both entities.)[5]

Jarvis Richards had purchased the Colorado ranch from Mr. and Mrs. Charles Kuhn ("Mr. and Mrs. Bohm" in this book). Kuhn, born in Pennsylvania in 1836, had taught school in the East before coming west and settling in Elbert County in the early 1870s. His XK Ranch on East Bijou Creek was located at a spot known as Kuhn's Crossing northwest of Simla, which was on the Rock Island Railroad to Colorado Springs. (The Union Pacific crossed the northeastern part of the county en route to Denver.)[6]

It was this ranch that newlywed Clarice Richards ("Esther Brook") first glimpsed and later wrote about in *A Tenderfoot Bride*. Her work calls to mind other "brides' books" such as Nannie T. Alderson and Helena Huntington Smith's *A Bride Goes West* and Harriet Fish Backus's *Tomboy Bride,* in which a naïve and inexperienced new wife confronts the challenges of making a home on the frontier. In Clarice Richards's account, however, the emphasis is not so much on her own culinary or housekeeping successes or catastrophes, for the upper-class Richardses obviously had help, but on the wider world of the ranch.

Yet Clarice's ladylike narrative is both more controversial and more complex than it might appear at first glance. For example, her portrayal of Charles Kuhn later drew criticism from other settlers, according to Elbert County historian Ethel Rae Corbett. Some felt, Corbett wrote in her *Western Pioneer Days,* that "his true character is sadly distorted. . . .

He was no such villian [*sic*] as the woman depicted. William Reilly, who was in the general merchandise business in Kiowa for many years, said that Mr. Kuhn was one of the best county treasurers the county ever had."[7]

Moreover, the book only briefly touches on the complicated issues involved in the courtroom battle between Jarvis Richards and a neighboring rancher. Concerning as it did the crucial questions of fencing and the use of the public domain, the altercation had its roots in the decades-long dispute among cattlemen large and small, farmers, and the federal government. Beginning with the passage of the Homestead Act in 1862, settlers had begun to pour onto the Great Plains, long the primary domain of the cattleman. Ranchers tried to control the range on which their cattle grazed, and in the process they often fenced in public lands as well as their own. In 1885 the government had ordered all illegal fences removed, but the issue remained. When Theodore Roosevelt became president in 1901, cattlemen assumed that, as an old Dakota rancher, he would be sympathetic to their interests. Instead, the president upheld the 1885 antifencing law, prompting some cattlemen to work for legislation to permit the leasing of the public domain. By 1902 Bartlett Richards was leading this fight (unresolved until the passage of the 1934 Taylor Grazing Act), even as his brother Jarvis was defending his own interests in court.[8]

In a suit that came to trial in the Arapahoe County District Court in Denver in 1902, John Sanderson, the plaintiff, accused Jarvis of driving his cattle off the range on which they had grazed previously. The area included land owned by both parties as well as public domain alternating with sections of former railroad land now part of the Richards ranch; to reach the government land, cattle had to cross unfenced

Richards property. At issue, therefore, was whether or not Richards could protect his own unenclosed land from Sanderson's cattle.

In his complaint, Sanderson alleged that, beginning about May 27, 1901, and continuing through September, Richards had by his actions either killed the cattle, poisoned them, or prevented them from breeding. Richards countered with testimony that his cowboys had gently and carefully driven off the cattle. The case was reported extensively in the Denver newspapers; the *Post* saw it as "in reality a fight between the small and the large cattlemen, the plaintiffs representing hundreds of small cattle owners similarly situated." As Clarice Richards writes, the judgment went against her husband. Ironically, Jarvis apparently ended up with the Sanderson property, according to Bartlett Richards. "He bought the John Sanderson land and has had the state locate him lands on the alternate sections between the railway sections he now owns," Bartlett wrote to his wife, Inez, in 1905. "So his land matters are about ended, I fancy. Fine, isn't it?"[9]

For Bartlett Richards himself, however, life was not so fine by 1905. In that year he and Will Comstock pleaded guilty to fencing violations in the Omaha federal district court. The next year they were charged with perjury and conspiracy in connection with allegedly fraudulent land filings. Found guilty, they appealed, but the verdicts were upheld. In late 1910, Bartlett Richards was imprisoned in Hastings, Nebraska, where he died in 1911, shortly before the end of his term.[10]

Beginning in 1907, while Bartlett was fighting his legal battles, Jarvis and Clarice Richards were spending most of their time in Denver, where Jarvis was involved with business investments and Clarice took part in various civic and social activities. During World War I, for example, she headed the Surgical Dressings Department of the Denver Red Cross chapter. In addition, in 1917 she was accepted into the Denver Fortnightly Club, an elite group founded in 1881 whose members included many of the city's most socially prominent women. Fortnightly members presented papers to the group on a regular basis and had supported such causes as the establishment of the Denver Public Library. For several years Clarice served as Fortnightly treasurer, and she was also the club's delegate to the General Federation of Women's Clubs.[11]

Moreover, Clarice Richards also was writing her "tales from an old ranch," published initially by the Fleming H. Revell Company in 1920. In assessing the work, *Bookman* noted that when she had arrived in Colorado, "it was still a lawless, pioneer land, with cattle, cowboys, and desperadoes . . . . She has caught them all in passing, and portrayed them to the life." The American Library Association's *Booklist* thought that the "rare charm" of the book came from the author's "growth through the delights and trials of existence among elemental conditions to a broad vision of life and its responsibilities." Four years later, *A Tenderfoot Bride* was reissued by Doubleday, Page and Company. On this occasion, the *New York Times* reviewer called the book a "welcome addition to the files of Americana" and congratulated the author for presenting "a truer picture of ranch life in the West than a dozen or more 'Western stories' bearing all too plainly the 'dime novel' brand."[12]

That Clarice's literary interests were more wide-ranging is demonstrated in a *Denver Post* article that appeared the same year *A Tenderfoot Bride* was first published. Indicating that she had been at work on another project, the paper described her recently completed manuscript "on the Aztec legends and those of the Ute tribes, and the legend of the beginning of the race of American Indians." Accompanying the article was a portrait of the author under the headline "Mrs. Clarice E. Richards, Noted Research Worker, Completes Book of Myth Translations, Which Says Hebrews Were Forefathers of Indians."[13]

After *A Tenderfoot Bride* came out, Clarice continued with her social and professional life in Denver. By 1923–24 the Denver *Social Record and Club Annual* listed her memberships as the Denver Allied Arts Association, the Denver Woman's Press Club, and the Denver Motor Club, in addition to Fortnightly. Her contributions to Fortnightly from 1920 through 1924 included papers entitled "Echoes of the Past," "Our Heritage," and "The Valley of the Second Sons" (about the Wet Mountain Valley of Colorado), later published in the *Colorado Magazine* of the State Historical Society.[14]

By the mid-1920s, however, the Richardses were living at least part of the time in Elbert County, where Jarvis was involved in "farm mortgages and farm lands for sale." In December 1928 he died in Seattle while visiting relatives; the *Denver Post* obituary noted that he was survived by his widow, a "widely known novelist."[15]

After her husband's death, Clarice Richards resided in Ward, a small mountain mining town west of Boulder, at the Lodge of the Pines, a guest ranch she had built in 1925 in partnership with a woman named Edna Howard. Although she apparently resigned from most of her Denver clubs, she did keep up her membership in Fortnightly and regularly presented papers until shortly before her death. For a time she also served as the housemother of the Kappa Kappa Gamma sorority at the University of Colorado in Boulder. She died in Denver in 1949 after becoming ill on a California vacation trip. Calling her "a Colorado social leader and authority on western history," the *Denver Post* noted in her obituary that she "was a student of Indian lore and art, and owned an outstanding collection of western literature." She was buried in Dayton, Ohio, in the family plot.[16]

Today her primary legacy remains *A Tenderfoot Bride*. Reflecting a rancher's perspective, the book portrays the turn-of-century "cow-punchers" and other diverse characters who would soon disappear forever, even as it provides a glimpse into a small part of the far-flung empire of the Richards brothers. The story traces, as well, the evolution of one woman from a "tenderfoot" to a "dyed-in-the-wool Westerner." In observing the changes taking place all around her, Clarice Richards herself had been changed forever.

Notes

1. Jarvis Richards, obituary, *Denver Post,* December 11, 1928, p. 18; obituary, *Dartmouth Alumni Magazine* 21 (February 1929): 256; biography, *General Catalogue of the Theological Seminary, Andover, Massachusetts, 1808–1909* (Boston: Thomas Todd, 1909), p. 416; Bartlett Richards, Jr., with Ruth Van Ackeren, *Bartlett Richards, Nebraska Sandhills Cattleman* (Lincoln: Nebraska State Historical Society, 1980), 32–33, 37.

2. Richards and Van Ackeren, *Bartlett Richards,* 3, 55–62, maps following 16; see also map in Mari Sandoz, *Old Jules* (1935; reprint, Lincoln: University of Nebraska Press, 1985), between pp. 25–26.

3. Richards and Van Ackeren, *Bartlett Richards,* 34–36, 50–51; Harry B. Henderson, Sr., "Governors of the State of Wyoming: DeForest Richards," *Annals of Wyoming* 12 (April 1940): 121–23.

4. Jarvis Richards, obituary, *Dartmouth Alumni Mag-*

azine; biography, *General Catalogue of the Theological Seminary,* 416; Mari Sandoz, *The Cattlemen: From the Rio Grande across the Far Marias* (New York: Hastings House, 1958), 432; Richards and Van Ackeren, *Bartlett Richards,* 79–80.

5. Jarvis Richards, obituary, *Dartmouth Alumni Magazine*; Richards and Van Ackeren, *Bartlett Richards,* 35, 75–76, 79, 94, 267 n.9.

6. Ethel Rae Corbett, *Western Pioneer Days: Biographies and Genealogies of Early Settlers with History of Elbert County, Colorado* (Denver, 1974), 98–99.

7. Ibid., 99.

8. Richards with Van Ackeren, *Bartlett Richards,* 99–112.

9. *John P. Sanderson* v. *Jarvis Richards and the Bijou Ranch Company,* Arapahoe County District Court, Denver, no. 33544, Colorado State Archives and Records Service, Denver; *Denver Post,* June 12, 1902, p. 10; Bartlett Richards to Inez Richards, November 26, 1905, printed in Richards and Van Ackeren, *Bartlett Richards,* 152.

10. Richards and Van Ackeren, *Bartlett Richards,* 140–45, 167–77, 194–221, passim.

11. Jarvis Richards, biography, *General Catalogue of the Theological Seminary,* 416; Clarice Richards, obituary, *Denver Post,* April 1, 1949, p. 16; *Social Record and Club Annual,* Denver, 1919–20; Robert L. Perkin, "Fortnightly Club to Note 75th Anniversary," *Rocky Mountain News,* May 20, 1956, p. 66; Yearbooks, 1919–25, Denver Fortnightly Club, Colorado Historical Society, Denver.

12. *Bookman,* December 1920, and *Booklist,* December 1920, quoted in Mary Katharine Reely and Pauline H. Rich, eds., *The Book Review Digest: Reviews of 1920 Books* (New York: H. W. Wilson Co., 1921), 448–49; *New York Times Book Review,* March 30, 1924, p. 25.

13. *Denver Post,* June 13, 1920, p. 9.

14. "List of Papers," Denver Fortnightly Club Papers, Western History Department, Denver Public Library; "The

Valley of the Second Sons," *The Colorado Magazine* 9 (July 1932): 140–46.

15. See the Denver *Social Record and Club Annual,* 1924–25, 1925–26; Jarvis Richards, obituary, *Denver Post,* December 11, 1928, p. 18.

16."List of Papers," Denver Fortnightly Club Papers; Clarice Richards obituary, *Denver Post,* April 1, 1949, p. 16.

I

FIRST IMPRESSIONS

WHEN our train left Colorado Springs and headed out into those vast stretches of the prairie, which spread East like a great green ocean from the foot of Pike's Peak, all the sensations of Christopher Columbus setting sail for a new world, and a few peculiarly my own, mingled in my breast.

As the train pounded along I stole a look at Owen. He was absorbed in the contemplation of a map of our new holdings. Under that calm exterior I suspected hidden attributes of the primitive man. Certainly there was some reason why Western life was to his liking, having had the chance to choose.

It was late in the afternoon when we found ourselves on the platform of the solitary little wayside station. The train went rushing on through the July sunshine, as if impatient at the stop. Our fellow passengers had drawn their heads back from the car windows, after vainly trying to see what apparently sane people could find to stop for in a place like that. In truth, there was little—a water tank, a section house, two cottages and one store.

A combination station-agent and baggage-man stood on the platform. Near a hitching rack a tall individual was waving his long arms about like a windmill as he beckoned us to approach. Owen picked up the bags; I trudged along behind with various coats and packages, stopping midway between platform and wagon to disengage a large tumbleweed, which had rolled merrily to my feet and attached itself to my skirt.

The tall man took a few steps in our direction, still holding the reins in his hand. With one eye he gave us a greeting, while he kept the other on the lunging horses. He was hardly a prepossessing person at first sight, except for his smile. I felt that his keen black eyes had sized us up in one quick glance. I became blushingly conscious of being a new bride, and from "the East."

"How-de-do? Whoa, now, Brownie. Just get in folks,—the old man had to go to town, so he sent me to meet you, but he'll be back by the time we get to the ranch." All this in one breath, while he helped Owen place the bags in the wagon.

"Don't mind the horses; they're plumb gentle—just a little ex-cited now over the train, that's all. Whoa now," with decided emphasis. "Sorry, Mrs. Brook, hope you didn't hurt yourself"—this last as the horses suddenly backed and knocked my foot off the step. "Oh, no, not at all," I replied, hastily scrambling into the wagon and thanking heaven that I had landed on the seat before they gave an unexpected lurch forward. Owen got in beside the driver; the horses reared and started off. I gripped the seat and my hat, and fastened my eyes on the horses' ears. When we had crossed the railroad and the movement was more steady, I began to "take notice" of things about me, and the conversation going on in the front seat reached me in fragments.

The driver said he was called "Tex." He was a true son of Texas, and it was not difficult to imagine that particles of his native soil still clung to him. The deep creases in his neck were so filled with dirt that he looked like a charcoal sketch. As he turned his face, lined and seamed, I saw that his chin was covered with at least a week's growth of greyish-black beard. I estimated his age. He might have been fifty; very quick in speech and action, yet there was a subdued power about the man. He managed the horses easily, and I caught in his drawling speech a casual, half-bantering tone.

"Wonder if them grips is botherin' the Missus. Ridin' all right?" he asked, turning with solicitude to see the location of the bags. As it happened, they were all located on top of my feet. It was Owen who removed them, for Tex's attention was again engaged with Brownie, who suddenly landed quite outside the road. A cotton-tail had jumped from behind a rattleweed.

"Quit that now, Brownie. You never did have no sense." The drawl was half-sarcastic. " 'Pears like you ain't never seen no rabbits before, 'stead a bein' raised with 'em." Brownie gave a little shake of her pretty head and crowded her long-suffering mate back into the road again. I was becoming very much interested. This man was a distinctly new type to me. I did not know then that he was the old-time cowpuncher, with an ease of manner a Chesterfield might have envied, and an unfailing, almost deferential, courtesy toward women.

Never shall I forget that first drive across the prairie,—not a house, not a tree in sight, except where the cottonwoods traced the borders of a waterless creek. Gently rolling hills were all about us, instead of the flat country I had expected to see; hills which failed to reveal anything when we reached the top, but yet higher hills to climb. An unexpected vastness seemed to extend to the very boundaries of the unknown, as we looked about on all sides, only to see the soft green circle of the hills, on which the bluest of skies gently rested, sweep about us. I felt the spell of unlimited space, and smiled as I thought of the tearful farewell of one of my bridesmaids. She had "hated" to think of my being "cooped up on a ranch." "Cooped up" here, when for the first time I realized what unhampered freedom might mean in a country left as God had made it, with so little trace of man's interference!

At last we came to a gate made of three strands of barbed wire, fastened together in the middle and attached to a stick at each end. It was a real gate when up, but when opened, it was a floppy invention of the Evil One, designed to tax the patience of a saint. The strands of wire got mixed and crossed and grew perceptibly shorter, so that it required superhuman strength and something of a disposition to get the end of the stick through the loop of wire, which held it in place again.

This gate marked the Southern boundary of the ranch, ten miles from the railroad station. We reached the top of a hill and looked up a long valley, where the creek wound its way, fringed by great cottonwood trees, until its source was lost behind three prominent buttes, purple in the haze of the late afternoon. Beyond the buttes stood Pike's Peak, snow-capped and alone, guardian of the valley, the whole length of which it commanded. Through some peculiarity of position all the other peaks of the Rockies remained invisible, while this one mountain rose in majestic isolation from the plain.

Tex stopped the horses for a moment, and without a word pointed with the whip toward a clump of cottonwoods in the distance.

"The ranch?" I asked.

He nodded.

In the beautiful valley it stood, the white fences, corrals and outbuildings gleaming in the sun. Nestled among the trees, planted so densely that only a suggestion of its white walls showed between them, was the house—our first home!

As we drove up to the gate, a short man, with a thick beard, bustled out to meet us.

"Well, here you are! Got here all right. Sorry I couldn't meet you. Come right in. You must be tired settin'." And before we quite realized that we had arrived, we were ushered into the house through the back door.

As a matter of fact, there was no front door. Two outside doors opened into the kitchen, one on either side, and since the kitchen was in truth the "living-room," what need of a front door?

A placid-faced, elderly woman greeted us, and after a few moments conducted us up a crooked stairway to a room under the eaves.

Owen left hastily "to look around outside," and I followed as quickly as possible for I knew that if I looked around inside for any length of time, I should start back to the railroad station on foot.

Old Mr. and Mrs. Bohm had lived on the place for over thirty years in this house, which was the evolution of a dug-out, with many subsequent periods in prospect before it became a possible home. Mrs. Bohm had recently been having "fainting spells," which frightened her husband into a plan to dispose of the ranch and live in town.

It was a wonderful ranch. Acres on acres of richest grass, a wealth of hay land and natural water holes,—a paradise for stock. To poor homesick me, this place had no suggestion of paradise. It looked run down and disorderly; the fences around the house were adorned with everything from old battered tin buckets and mowing-machine wheels to the smallest piece of rusty wire. Mrs. Bohm confided to me that "James liked it that way because everything was so handy." There was no questioning that, but as a first impression it was hopeless, and my heart grew heavier and heavier as I thought of the new house in Wyoming, where we had expected to be, and the Eastern home I had just left.

I walked out of sight of the festooned fence and tried to think. Up the valley the Peak was deep blue against the golden evening sky, and in the vast, unbroken silence of the prairies I felt the sense of chaos and confusion give way to peace. The old house, tumble-down fences, m o w i n g machine wheels and wire took an inconsequent place in the scale of things compared to Owen's undertaking. He *must* succeed. The undesirable could be removed or made over.

We were in a new world, we had a great domain, we faced undreamed of experiences and possibilities. My spirits rose with a bound, and I resolved from that moment to consider our life here in the West, in the midst of new conditions, a great adventure. At that instant the original Bohm dug-out would have held no terrors for me.

Perhaps if I had known just how great the adventure was to be, what varied and nerve-testing experiences the future did hold, I might have been daunted; but with a farewell look at the Peak and a new sense of strength and courage, I went to meet Owen. I realized that he knew the possibilities of the place and that the conditions would all soon be changed, and I knew, too, that he was distressed at the realization of how it must all appear to me. He looked troubled, as he came toward me.

"Can you stand it for a little while?" he asked.

"Of course, I can," I replied, cheerfully, blindly taking the first step toward the great adventure.

"It's all right, dear; it's going to be wonderful, living here."

Mr. and Mrs. Bohm, Tex and six bashful cow-punchers were in the kitchen waiting for us before they sat down to supper. We were presented to the men, and in acknowledgment of the introduction received a fleeting glance from six pairs of diffident eyes and a quick jerk from six slickly brushed heads.

Mrs. Bohm took her seat at the foot of the long oil-cloth-covered table, and old Mr. Bohm sat at the head. Fortunate for me that Owen and I sat side by side. If once during that meal I had caught his eye, I should have disgraced myself forever.

Except old Bohm, no one said anything. Indeed, no one had a chance, for he talked all the time, telling stories, cracking jokes at which he laughed immoderately, interspersing his conversation with waves of his fork, with which from time to time he reflectively combed his beard. I could not take my eyes off him; there was a weird fascination in following the movements of that fork.

It was prescience which led me to do so, for old Bohm suddenly ceased using it as a toilet article and jabbed it into a piece of meat, which he held out toward me.

"Here, Mrs. Brook, have some more beef. I've been talkin' along here and clean forgot you folks must be hungry." I assured him I couldn't eat another bite. It was the most truthful statement of my life.

That night I laid awake for hours, thinking over the day's experiences, and incidentally trying to find a spot on the mattress where a lump did not threaten to press a rib out of place. At last I fell asleep, to be suddenly awakened by the slam of a gate under our window, followed by an exclamation which floated up out of the grey dawn: "By hell, but this is a fine day." Then came the squeak of the pump handle, as old Bohm performed his morning ablutions, more slams of the gate, and more salutations of the same order in varying phraseology, but always beginning with "By hell."

Shades of my ministerial ancestors! Was this the language of the new country in

which we had come to live? Surely the
great adventure promised startling sensations at the outset, to say nothing of a certain sliding scale of standards.

Owen stirred and asked sleepily what on
earth I was doing up at that hour of the
day.

"Changing my viewpoint," I replied, looking out toward old Bohm's shadowy figure
on its way toward the corral. "That has to
be done early."

II

A SURPRISE PARTY

WE were living in the land of the unexpected. Six weeks on the ranch demonstrated that. The possibilities for surprise were inexhaustible, and the probabilities innumerable and certain, if Owen happened to be away.

On one of these occasions the cook eloped with the best rider on the place, more thrilling and upsetting to my peace of mind than the cloud-burst and flood that followed soon after. Twenty-two husky and hungry men wanted three square meals a day, and one inexperienced bride stood between them and starvation. The situation was mutually serious.

In my need came help. Tex, our coachman on that first drive, saved the day. Shortly after the elopement he came in for supplies for the cow-camp. I was almost

© By Permission W. G. Walker

ROPING AND CUTTING OUT CATTLE

hidden by pans of potatoes, and was paring away endlessly. He was very quiet when I explained, but after supper he gathered up the dishes to wash them for me, looking very serious. When he had finished, he suddenly turned to me:

"Say, Mrs. Brook, I've just been studyin'. Jack Brent kin cook for the boys out at camp all right, and if you kin stand it, I kin come in and cook for you. It sure got my goat to see you rastlin' with them potatoes and wearin' yourself out cookin' for these here men."

Good old Tex! That was little short of saintly. Camp cooking where he was autocrat was far more to his taste. He hated "messin' 'round where there was women," as he expressed it. Here was sacrifice indeed! Tex scrubbed his hands until they fairly bled, enveloped himself in a large checked gingham apron, and proceeded to act as chef until the eloper had been replaced.

Something deepened in me. I was seeing a new thing.

Owen had been gone nearly a week. One morning I happened to be in the kitchen when Mrs. Bohm entered. Casually she asked Tex whether Ed More's wife had left him before he went to jail, or after he got out. Half in joke, I said:

"Mercy, Mrs. Bohm, is there a man in this country, with the exception of Tex, who hasn't been in jail or on the way there?"

I was interrupted by the slamming of a door, and Tex had vanished. Mrs. Bohm looked embarrassed as she replied:

"I just hate to tell you, Mrs. Brook, and Tex would feel terrible to have you know; but you say such queer things sometimes, I'd better tell you now that Tex"—she paused a moment—"he's only been out of the 'pen' himself a year."

"Tex in the penitentiary? What on earth for?" I was almost dazed.

"Well, I'll tell you." Mrs. Bohm began the story with apparent reluctance, but her manner soon betrayed a certain zest. "You see, about four years ago Tex was workin' for a man up on Crow Creek and took some cattle on to Omaha to sell for him. When he came back he never brought a cent of money, and told how he had been held up and robbed. Everybody believed it at first, then all to onct his family—they live over West—began to dress to kill, and Tex bought brass beds for every room in the house; then folks began to suspicion where he got the money, and he was sent to the Pen for two years."

Poor old Tex! Who would ever have supposed a secret longing for brass beds would prove his undoing? I might have guessed horses or cards, but never brass beds. I almost felt the breath of tragedy. She seemed sweeping by.

Mrs. Bohm went on: "Tex's mighty good to his family, though, and it most killed him when his wife went off with a Mexican sheep-herder while he was doin' time. She's back home now with the girls, but her and Tex's separated. Ain't it a fright the way women acts?"

"It certainly is," I agreed, trying to reconcile my previous idea of convicts with having one for a cook. It was dreadfully confusing and disturbing. In spite of what I had just heard, I knew I trusted Tex. He would never steal from us, I felt sure. And my instinct told me he would be a true and loyal friend. There was no apparent excuse for what he had done, but he had paid for his moment of weakness more fully perhaps than anyone realized. I pondered over it.

Presently he came in, with a curious, troubled expression on his face. I gave him the orders, as usual, with no sign of having heard of the cloud under which he had lived for three miserable years. Our relations were re-established. I could see his relief.

We were still taking our meals in the kitchen, although the house was gradually being remodeled. It was Saturday evening, and we were expecting Owen home. There was an air of suppressed excitement among the men. One, and then another, bolted from the table and out of the door, returning in a shame-faced manner to explain that he "thought he heered somethin'." Certainly Owen's coming would never produce such a sensation, unless he was expected to arrive in an airship. I was more than ever mystified.

After the meal was over, there was such a general shaving—also in the kitchen—and such donning of red neckties, that I could not restrain my curiosity. I called Tex aside and asked him where they were going. He looked a little sheepish, as he replied:

"Why, we ain't goin' nowhere." Then in a burst of confidence, "I don't know as I'd orter tell you, but the fact is, you folks is goin' to be surprised; all the folks 'round is goin' to have a party here, and we're expectin' 'em."

I gasped. A sudden suspicion flashed through my mind.

"Tex, did you plan this? What on earth shall I do?"

Tex saw I was really troubled. "Why, Mrs. Brook," he said, "you don't have to do nothin'. Just turn the house over to 'em, and along about midnight I'll make some coffee—they'll bring baskets."

I was relieved to know that they only

wanted the house, and would provide their own refreshments, for it was appalling to be an impromptu hostess to an entire community and to speculate upon the possibility of one small cold roast and chocolate cake satisfying a crowd of young people, after drives of thirty miles or more across the prairie.

"Me and the boys"—Tex spoke somewhat apologetically, as he started toward the door—"we kind a thought maybe you and Mr. Brook would like to get acquainted, seein's how you're goin' to live here; but I guess we oughten to have did what we done."

I felt ashamed of my momentary perturbation, as the force of that last sentence of Tex's reached me. These men of the plains were as simple and sensitive as children about many things. They would really grieve if they felt this affair, planned solely on our account, gave us no pleasure. I hastened to reassure him.

"It was mighty nice of you men to think of it," I said, cheerfully. "We do want to know the people in the country, and we are going to enjoy every moment. I was 'surprised' before the party began, that's all."

Tex went out satisfied, grinning broadly.

To my good fortune, Owen arrived before the guests came. I told him what was about to befall us. His expression was dubious. All he said was "Thunder."

Owen and one of the men had been driving about the country all the week, buying horses suitable to turn in on a Government cavalry contract. The night before they had spent on the floor of a cold railroad station, wrapped up in their blankets, with a lighted lantern under the covering at their feet. Their sleep was somewhat broken, with either cremation or freezing pending that cold September night. Poor Owen! He was completely worn out. And now he had to go through a surprise party.

At eight o'clock, Tex, self-appointed master of ceremonies, ushered in the first arrivals. They were a tall, lean chap and two very much be-curled young misses. I made trials without number at conversation, but they could only be induced to say "Yes" and "No."

From eight until ten they came,—ranch-men, cow-punchers, ex-cow-punchers running their own outfits, infant cow-punchers, girls and women, until kitchen and sitting room were filled to overflowing, and every chair and bench on the place in use. Among the last to arrive was a tall, languid Texan, accompanied by two languid, drab-colored women. They were presented to us as "Robert, Missus Reed and Maggie." "Maggie," I immediately concluded, was a sister, but not being quite certain, I sought enlightenment from Mrs. Bohm.

"She ain't Reed's sister," she informed me in a low tone, "she's his girl."

"Oh, works for them, you mean?" I said, somewhat puzzled by the Reed connections.

"Works nothin'," Mrs. Bohm replied, scornfully. "She's got the next place to 'em and goes with 'em everywhere. Ella don't seem to mind. I'd just call her 'Maggie' if I was you," and Mrs. Bohm departed to join a group of women near the door.

I looked over at the two with a new interest. They were chatting and laughing

together, the "girl" and the wife seemingly
on the best of terms, with no sign of rivalry
for the tall Texan's affections. Here was a
situation fraught with latent possibilities
that made me tremble, yet—"Ella don't
seem to mind."

The kitchen had been converted into a
ballroom by moving the table up against the
wall and placing three chairs upon it. Un-
fortunately the sink and stove were fixtures,
but everything else, including the bread jar,
found a temporary resting place in the yard.

Old Bohm, with his fiddle under his arm,
gingerly ascended the table first. Then another man followed with a similar instru-
ment; and last came a youth with a mouth
harp. No fatality having resulted from the
musicians taking their seats, the dancing
began.

The music, if such a combination of sounds
can be dignified by that name, was such as
to defy description. Never in the wildest
flights of fancy could I have conceived of
such execution and such sounds. The two
men sawed their violins, and the third was

purple in the face from his efforts on the mouth-harp; all were stamping time with their feet, and he of the harp was slapping his knee with his unoccupied hand.

Before every dance a council was held, after which each musician would play the tune decided upon, as best suited to his taste. Old Bohm tried to get to the end in the shortest time possible, while the second fiddler, taking things more seriously, finished four or five bars behind his companion. The harpist, not playing "second" to anything or anybody, had his own opinion as to how "A Hot Time in the Old Town" should go. With these independent views, the result was a series of the most discordant sounds that ever fell on mortal ears. However, music mattered little, for all had come to have a good time, and the "caller-out," with both eyes shut tight and arms folded across his breast, was making himself heard above all other sounds.

"Birdie in the center and all hands around!" he commanded. Then fiddles and mouth harp began a wild jig, couples raced 'round and 'round, while "Birdie," a blond and blushing maiden, stood patiently in the midst of the whirling circle, until the next order came:

> "Birdie hop out and Crow hop in!
> Take holt of paddies and run around agin."

"Crow" was a broad, heavy-set cow-puncher, wearing chaps, and in the endeavor to "run around agin," I found my progress somewhat impeded by his spurs, which caught in my skirt and very nearly upset me.

All the riders wore their heavy boots and spurs, and it required real agility to avoid being stepped on or having one's skirt torn to ribbons. I was devoutly thankful that chiffon and tulle ball gowns were not worn on ranches.

There was more to avoid than spurs. We had to dance about the kitchen and avoid the stove, the sink and the tabled musicians, to say nothing of the nails in the floor. But after a few hours' practice, I began to feel qualified to waltz on top of the House of the Seven Gables, and avoid at least six of them.

Finally, the caller-out shouted loudly:

"Allemande, Joe! Right hand to pardner and
      around you go.
Balance to corners, don't be slack;
Turn right around and take a back track.
When you git home, don't be afraid,
Swing her agin and all promenade."

My partner obeyed every command with
such vigor that when at last he led me to
my seat I was panting and dizzy; nor had I
quite recovered my breath when the music
struck up again, and Tex led me forth.

The exertion of the first quadrille had been
too much for his comfort, so he had dispensed with both collar and coat. His
trousers and vest bore evidence of having
seen many a round-up, and his shirt, which
had once been white, was now multi-colored.
In the wonderful red ascot tie which encircled his neck were stuck four scarfpins, one
above the other. There being nothing to
hold the loop of the tie in place, it gradually
worked up the back of his head, until its
progress was stopped by the edge of a small
skull-cap, which Tex wore as the crowning
feature of his costume. The cap, tilted

slightly to one side, gave him a rakish appearance, quite in contrast with his air of importance and responsibility.

I danced—my head fairly spins when I think *how* I danced—for, since the party was given in our honor, dance I must with every man who asked me.

Owen, not being a dancing man, made himself agreeable to the wall-flowers and the children, stealing upstairs about once an hour for a few moments' nap on the bedroom floor. The beds themselves were occupied by sleeping infants, whose mothers were going through the intricate mazes of those dances below.

At one o'clock Tex began to make the coffee, whereupon the musicians descended from the table, and the expectant party sat down. But where were their baskets? My heart sank, as Tex approached holding a very small one. He informed me in a stage whisper it was all there was!

The basket contained a cake and one wee chick, evidently fried soon after leaving the shell. It was the smallest chicken I ever saw. I hastily produced our cake and roast, and then took one despairing look around at the forty individuals to be fed. I shall never be able to explain it, unless Tex had an Aladdin's lamp concealed in his pocket, for cake, roast and chicken appeared to be inexhaustible, and the supply more than equaled the demand.

I was aroused from my contemplation of the miracle by a feminine voice, the speaker saying half to herself and half to me:

"It took me most two hours to iron Nell's dress this mornin', but I sure got a pretty 'do' on it." Following her beaming glance, I found that it rested on a mass of ruffles, which adorned the dress of "Birdie" of that first quadrille. Just then the music began again, and I saw Ed Lay ask her to dance. I trusted, after all that work, the 'do' wouldn't be undone by his spurs; still the effort had not been wasted, for this was the fifth time he had danced with her.

No doting mother could have taken more pride in the debut of an only child, than this work-worn sister whose eyes sparkled as they followed "Birdie's" whirling figure held firmly by the encircling arm of the cow-puncher, and she murmured softly with a half sigh, "Ain't it grand?" To me it was "grand" indeed, that even an embryo romance could bring a new light to those tired eyes.

It was six o'clock Sunday morning when one most thoughtful person suggested that "they'd orter be goin'"; and by seven the last guest had departed. Then Owen and I, weary and heavy-eyed, donned our wraps, climbed into the wagon, and started on a sixteen-mile drive to the railroad to meet his brother, who was coming from California to see "how we were making it."

I was almost too tired to speak, but one thought was struggling for expression, and as we started up the first long hill, I had to say:

"Anyone who ever spoke of the 'peace and quiet of ranch life' lived in New York and dreamed about it. In twenty-four hours I have discovered that we have an ex-convict for a trusted cook, and have received as guests a man with his wife and resident affinity. We have had a surprise party and I have danced with all the blemished characters the country boasts of, until six o'clock in the morning of the Sabbath day, with never a qualm of conscience. What do you suppose has become of my moral standards?"

Owen was amused. He asked me, quizzically, what I thought they would be by the end of a year.

"Mercy!" I replied, "at the rate they are being overthrown, there won't be enough left to consider, unless"—I thought a moment—"unless I can reconstruct a more enduring set from parts of the old."

III

THE ROOT CELLAR

"FOR East is East and West is West, and never the twain shall meet." The phrase kept haunting me all through these first days when everything was so new and strange. I almost felt as though I had passed into a new phase of existence.

Except for Owen, there was no point of contact between the world of cities and people I had just left and this land of cattle and cow-punchers, bounded by the sky-rimmed hills. In Owen, however, the East and the West did meet. He understood and belonged to both and adapted himself as easily to the one as to the other. Wearing his derby, he belonged to the life of the East; in his broad-brimmed Stetson, he was a living part of the West.

The compelling reality of this new life

41

affected me deeply. Non-essentials counted for nothing. There were no artificial problems or values.

No one in the country cared who you might have been or who you were. The *Mayflower* and Plymouth Rock meant nothing here. It would be thought you were speaking of some garden flowers or some breed of chickens.

The one thing of vital importance was what you were—how you adjusted yourself to meet conditions as you found them, and how nearly you reached, or how far you fell below their measure of man or woman.

I felt as though up to this time I had been in life's kindergarten, but that I had now entered into its school, and I realized that only as 1 passed the given tests should I succeed.

I learned much from the rough, untutored men with whom I was in daily association. They were men whose rules of conduct were governed by individual choice, unhampered by conventions. They were so direct and honest, so unfailingly kind and gentle toward any weaker thing, and so simple and responsive, that I liked and trusted them from the first.   All but old Bohm, the man from whom we were buying.   He was such a totally different type that he seemed a man apart.   The son of a German father and an Irish mother, he had inherited a nature too complex and contradictory to be easily fathomed.

Mrs. Bohm, with her white, calm face and gentle voice, attracted me, but her husband aroused in both Owen and me an instinctive distrust.   He was good nature personified, a most companionable person, with his easy, contagious laugh, his amusing stories, quick wit, and breezy air of good fellowship.   He could quote Burns, Scott, and other poets by the hour, and fiddle away on his violin, until we were nearly moved to tears.   He was almost too good-natured; he didn't quite ring true.   I noticed that while he always referred or spoke to his wife affectionately, as "my old mammy," her attitude toward him was rather impersonal.   She called him "James" with quiet dignity, but seldom talked with him, and appeared to take very little interest.

On the side of a hill, some distance from the house, was an old root cellar, used, according to Bohm, for storing potatoes, turnips, and other vegetables for winter. It was most inconveniently located; there were hillsides much nearer, and considering that the cellar under the house was always used for such purposes, it seemed strange that another should be needed so far away. I was possessed with a desire to explore it. It suggested hidden treasures and Indian relics, which I was collecting.

One day I was poised on the top of the cellar step, about to descend into its mysterious depths.

Old Bohm appeared. "Was you lookin' for something'?" he asked, somewhat out of breath.

"Oh, no," I replied, going down a few steps. "I was just exploring, and thought I would investigate this old root cellar."

"I thought that was what you was goin' to do, and I hurried up to tell you to be

awful careful of rattlesnakes; there's a pile
of 'em 'round these here old cellars." Bohm
spoke with apparent solicitude.

"Heavens! I wouldn't go down there for
anything!" I exclaimed,—and I got out of
the cellarway as quickly as possible.

Old Bohm looked down the steps at the
strong, closed door of heavy boards.

"Oh, maybe it would be all right. You
could listen for 'em and jump, if you heard
'em rattle," he remarked, casually.

I shook my head. "Not much; I don't
want to hear them rattle," and I started
toward the house.

Bohm went up toward the wind-mill. As
I turned away I caught a curious expression
on his face—a faint gleam of something.

As I came through the meadow gate,
Owen was getting into the buggy.

"Hello," he called, "I've been looking for
you everywhere. I have to drive over to
Three Bar. Do you want to go?"

I was always ready to go anywhere, so
while Owen was driving the horses about, I
ran in to get my hat.

Not one of our horses was thoroughly broken, so we always had to follow the same method of procedure before starting anywhere. After the horses were hitched up, Charley, to whom fell odd jobs of every sort, stood at their heads until Owen was fairly seated and had the lines firmly in his hands. Then, after a few ineffectual attempts to kick or run down Charley before he could get out of the way, off dashed the horses around and around the open space between the house and the pond, until a little of the edge had been taken off their spirits. Then Owen stopped them for one moment, I made a quick jump into the buggy, and away we went at top speed toward the gate that Charley had run to open. We usually missed the post by a quarter of an inch, and at that juncture I invariably shut my eyes and held my breath.

The road to Three Bar Ranch led to the North and wound up a very long hill, then across a rolling mesa. The prairie was covered with short grama grass, just turning a faint brown, the yellow sunflowers and great clumps of rattleweed, with its spikes of lovely purple, giving a touch of color to the scene before us. The Spanish bayonet dotted the hillsides, and over all hung the summer sky like burnished copper. The only sound, aside from that of the horses' hoofs and the crunch of the wheels on the soft prairie road, was the occasional song of the meadow lark, all the joy of the summer day sounding in its one short thrilling note. In the gulches, where the grass grew deep and rank, the wind tossed it softly, and it rippled and sparkled in the shifting light, as water gleams in the sun. Everything was so still that animation seemed for the time suspended, as we drove along silenced by the spell of the prairies.

Three Bar, one of the oldest ranches in the country, stood against the side of a hill. It was a long, low structure of logs built in the prevailing fashion of the early ranch houses, room after room opening into one another, usually with an outside door to each.

The ranch was owned by the Mortons,

English people, who were among the earliest settlers in the country. They greeted us most cordially, and as Owen went out to the corral with Mr. Morton to look at some horses, Mrs. Morton took me into the house.

The room we entered had very little furniture, but was redeemed from bareness by a wonderful old stone fireplace at one end.

Mrs. Morton was short and heavy set. "Spotless" was the only word her appearance suggested when I first saw her. Her skin was as fair as a child's, while her hair was as white as the apron she wore.

Her flow of conversation was unceasing, and I was reminded of a remark that Charley made to me when the telephone was first put in over the fence lines.

"Old lady Morton talked so fast that she ripped all the barbs off the wire." Before I had time to reply to one question, she had asked another, and was off on an entirely different subject. I suppose the accumulated conversation of months was vented on my innocent head, for she told me, poor thing, that she hadn't seen another woman since Christmas.

"Us"—she never said we—"us never visits the neighbors, but was coming up to see you, Mrs. Brook, for us heard you and Mr. Brook was different. Us lives out here on a ranch, but us knows when people are the right kind."

I didn't know whether to be considered "different" was desirable, or not, and I was dying to ask her what constituted "the right kind," but had no time before she suddenly asked:

"Have the Bohms gone? Us was waiting till they went."

I explained that they were still on the ranch, as Mr. Bohm had to gather and counterbrand all the stock before turning it over to Owen, and that he had been delayed.

Mrs. Morton gave a little grunt of contempt. "Old Bohm won't hurry any while he's getting free board. He may be with you all winter. Us hopes Mr. Brook won't be imposed on. He's a smart man, old Jim Bohm is, but he's a bad one."

"Bad one?" I repeated, inwardly praying that the Bohms would not be permanent guests.

"Old Jim Bohm is a bad man," Mrs. Morton said again, rocking violently back and forth. "I was here when they came. She's all right, but there is nothing he won't do. Why"—her voice sank to a whisper—"sixteen men have been traced as far as that ranch and never been heard of again, and Jim Bohm's been getting richer all along."

Mrs. Morton scarcely paused for breath, so I couldn't have said anything. But I was speechless, anyhow.

"Not one of them, **not one**," she declared, "was ever heard of again, and if you were to examine that old root cellar on the hill, you'd find out what I say is true."

The incident of the morning flashed across my mind, and I felt as though a piece of ice were being drawn slowly along my spine.

"How perfectly horrible!" I managed to gasp, "but it can't be true."

"It's true, all right." There was no doubting Mrs. Morton's conviction. "There's facts there's no getting 'round. Jim Bohm and old Happy Dick, that used to work for him, came up here over the trail from Texas with a band of horses that Bohm and another man owned. The other fellow was with them when they started, but Bohm said he died on the way, and that's all anyone knows about it, except that old Bohm kept all the horses."

"Then a few years later, a young fellow that was consumptive, came out to work for them. I know he had quite a bit of money, because he stopped here once to ask John what to do with it. He hadn't been there very long before he dropped dead, according to Jim Bohm's story. His folks back East tried to get the money, but Bohm said the fellow owed it to him, and they couldn't do a thing about it."

I sat as if petrified, unable to take my eyes from Mrs. Morton's face, as she went on and on.

"He was in with all the rustlers in the country," she continued, "and once when a posse was hunting a man who had stole a lot of horses, Bohm tried his best to keep them from searching the place, but the Sheriff told him they would arrest him if he made any more fuss about it, so he had to keep still. When they came to the hay-mow, they stuck a pitchfork right into a man hidden in the hay, and old Bohm swore he didn't know a thing about his being there. The next us heard, old Bill Law had dropped dead in the corral. I tell you"— Mrs. Morton leaned forward and shook her finger in my face—"it's mighty funny, the way men keeps dropping dead over there; they don't do it anywhere else. Happy Dick was the last. About a year ago he told Morton he'd stole two men rich, and now he was going to steal himself rich. But two days after he was found dead in the willows, and Bohm said that when he came upon the body, Happy Dick had been dead for hours."

Mrs. Morton showed signs of running down for a moment, so I hastened to ask why it was that, though suspicion always pointed toward him, old Bohm had never been arrested.

© By Permission W. G. Walker

ROPING A STEER TO INSPECT BRAND

"Jim Bohm's too smooth," Mrs. Morton answered. "If you found him with a smoking gun in his hand and a man dead on the ground beside him, he'd lie out of it somehow; probably would swear that as he came up, he saw the man shoot himself. Oh! he's a slick one. Us always said us pitied anyone who had business dealings with him, but," she stopped as she saw Owen and Mr. Morton coming up the walk, "Mr. Brook looks like a man that can take care of himself. I'd watch out for Bohm, though. Watch out for him!"

"Thank you, Mrs. Morton," I said, as Owen came to the door. "I am glad you told me. Please come to see us," and with conflicting emotions I prepared to leave Three Bar Ranch.

I scarcely knew what to think. I was worried, and yet——

When I told Owen I expected him to pooh-pooh the story and relieve my mind, but he did nothing of the sort. With a queer little wrinkle between his eyes, he listened attentively.

"Owen, you don't think there is any truth in it, do you?" I asked, much troubled by his silence. He flicked a fly off Dan's back before replying:

"I don't know what to think. The old chap's a rascal, there's no doubt about that; but I didn't suppose he was a cold-blooded murderer."

Again I felt the ice go up and down my spine. "Great heavens, Owen, can't you have someone go through the root cellar, to see if there is anything out of the way there? And, above all, get the stock gathered and ship Bohm—I despise him, anyhow!"

"Don't let it worry you," said Owen; "probably it's all mere talk. Bohm won't bother us; and in a few weeks the stock will all be turned over and he'll have no excuse for staying."

"A few weeks is a long time," I said, gloomily, feeling as if my hold on life were gradually slipping. "According to Mrs. Morton, everybody on the place might drop dead in less time than that."

Owen laughed, but the next moment a

shadow crossed his face, and he said decisively:

"I'm going to look into that root-cellar business. I want to have the place thoroughly cleaned out, anyhow."

The boys were going in to supper when we drove up. Charley came to take the horses, and Owen greeted him:

"Well, how's everything?"

"Oh, all right," answered Charley indifferently, as he started to loosen the tugs. "Nothin's happened since you folks went away, only the old root cellar's caved in."

Speech was impossible. Owen and I stood as if petrified, looking at each other. We turned to go up to the house. I felt as though some wretched fate were making game of us. As we entered the door, Owen spoke:

"Esther"—he was very serious—"don't say a word or betray any interest whatever in this matter. After supper is over, I'll go up to investigate."

Talk about the skeleton at a feast! There

were sixteen horrid, grinning things around the table that night, besides a few that Mrs. Morton had overlooked.

Mrs. Bohm was whiter than usual and very quiet. Old Bohm was in high spirits. We were scarcely seated before he declared it "a damn shame" that the old root cellar had to cave in.

We showed a little surprise, but affected unconcern. Playing the role assigned to me, I remarked indifferently that we never used it, anyhow, and with this Bohm cheerfully agreed.

Later, when Owen went up to examine the cellar, I noticed, from my point of observation at the window, that old Bohm was close by his side.

Soon after Owen came in looking very grave.

"Well, it caved in, all right, and it never can be cleaned out. But there's one thing I am convinced of"—and he looked toward the hill with a frown—"it didn't cave in of itself."

IV

THE GREAT ADVENTURE PROGRESSES

JOHN, the mail carrier, was our only connecting link with the great outside world. Three times a week he brought the mail. From the first sight of a tiny speck on the top of the distant hill, our hearts thrilled. I watched it grow larger and larger, until the two-wheeled cart stopped at the garden gate. With hands trembling with impatience, I unlocked the old, worn bag, which John threw on the floor.

I was the honorable Postmistress. My desk was covered with Postal Laws, which I almost learned by heart. I had the New England respect for the Federal prison, the place of correction for delinquent Postal employees.

One rule was absolute. The key of the mail bag had to be securely attached to the Post Office. My Post Office was a wooden cracker box, which held the mail for the few outside patrons.

The inspector of Post Offices arrived unannounced one day. He frowningly looked over my accounts, while I stood by in perturbation. Suddenly he caught sight of the key at the end of a long brass chain "securely attached to the Post Office." He got up to investigate. The frown disappeared by magic, and a smile played around his stern mouth. He burst into laughter. I explained I was very careful to comply with all the regulations. He gave me a humorous glance—and stayed to dinner.

The papers on Monday evening brought us exciting news. A train on the U. P. had been held up at a lonely station, thirty miles from our ranch. All the Pullman passengers had been robbed and one man shot and killed. The hold-ups had escaped and were at large in the "country adjoining."

"If they are in the country adjoining, they'll come here eventually," I remarked to Owen. "This ranch is a perfect magnet for all the questionable characters in the vicinity."

Owen thanked me for the compliment and went out to the bunk house to interview Robert Reed, now in charge of the hay gang.

This Reed was an interesting fellow,—a natural leader of men, and so efficient that Owen had made him hay foreman.

When we had driven over to his claim to see him about working for us, Mrs. Reed came out to the buggy, wiping her hands on her apron.

"No, Bob ain't home this morning," she responded to Owen's inquiry for her husband. "I reckon you'll find him over ploughin' for Maggie." A statement made in the most matter-of-fact manner.

We drove over to another claim shack a mile or so from the Reeds', where Bob was indeed ploughing for Maggie. To him, too, it was quite a matter of course.

The affinity problem in this country really appeared simple. Mrs. Reed evidently accepted Maggie as a natural factor in the situation, and her marital relations were not disturbed in the least, as long as Bob finished his own ploughing first. That woman was truly oriental in her cast of mind.

Maggie Lane's mother and brother lived near at hand, also. One brother, Tom, was Reed's constant companion. Altogether it was a perfectly harmonious arrangement.

The Lane family records were not quite clear. Acquaintance revealed that. They all seemed to have a penchant for leaving the straight and narrow path for the broad highway of individual choice. Obviously Maggie's position did not affect her family, nor her social standing in the community.

Whenever I drove about the country without Owen, I took Charley with me on horseback. Gates were hard to open, and my team of horses was not thoroughly broken. Besides, there were always the possibilities of the unexpected on these lonely prairies. I called Charley my Knight of the Garter. When he knew in advance he was going with me, he went up to the bunkhouse "to slick up." If it chanced to be summer, he emerged without a coat, his blue shirt sleeves held up by a pair of beribboned pink garters, a pair of heavy stamped leather cuffs on his wrists, and a heavy stamped leather collar holding his neck like a vise.

I suggested one morning that the collar might be uncomfortably warm. He met my objection with scorn.

"Hot, Mrs. Brook? Why, that ain't hot. You see, the leather kinda ab-sorbs the sweat and makes it nice and cool."

One day we were out to take the washing to Mrs. Reed. I had asked Bob to take it Saturday night, when he and Tom Lane had "gone over home" to finish that ploughing. I supposed he had done so, but when he came back on Monday, he said he had "plumb forgot it, but would take it next time."

We had to pass through Maggie's claim on the way. She was standing at her door, as we stopped to open the gate. There was no freshly ploughed ground in sight, and I idly asked if she had finished her ploughing.

"No," she replied, "I kinda looked for Bob over Sunday to finish it, but I reckon he couldn't get off. I wish you'd tell him to stop here the next time he goes home."

We drove on, and I wondered what Maggie

"reckoned" he couldn't get away from,—the ranch or his wife.

I gave Mrs. Reed the clothes and I told her Bob had forgotten to bring them over with him Saturday. She looked at me curiously.

"Didn't Bob work Sunday?"

"No," I replied, "none of the men worked Sunday. Tom and Bob both said they were going home."

Mrs. Reed frowned.

"Oh, I suppose Maggie had somethin' she wanted him to do."

Charley started to answer, but my look stopped him.

"I'll have your clothes ready Saturday." Mrs. Reed slammed the gate and turned toward the house.

"Gee," said Charley, riding up close beside the buggy, "them two women'll be fightin' over Bob yet, if he ain't careful. Why, that's funny"—he looked at me questioningly,—"Bob wasn't to Maggie's, either, was he?"

"No," I answered, "I was just wondering

about that myself. Perhaps he went to town, instead." A coyote ran out of a gulch. Charley with a whoop started in pursuit, and the entire incident passed from my mind.

We were going in to supper, when three men drove up to the door. Whenever strangers appeared, I always had a moment of uncertainty as to whether they were to be sent to the bunkhouse with the men, or invited to our own table. Instantaneous social classification is rather difficult when there are no distinguishing external signs. And it had to be done at the moment. The men asked for Owen.

We had no idea who they were, so our conversation during supper was limited to impersonal topics, such as the present, past and future weather, the condition of the range and stock—nothing calculated to offend the delicate sensibilities of a Governor, a ranchman or an ex-convict, inasmuch as our guests might come under any of these heads. Entertaining on a ranch is democratic in the extreme.

They went out with Owen after supper.

From the window I could see four dim figures sitting on their heels by the corral gate, talking earnestly.

It was late when they drove away. I was putting up the mail, as Owen entered. His announcement drove all idea of the Postal Laws and regulations out of my head.

"Well, they've gone, and have taken Bob and Tom Lane with them."

"Mercy! what for? Who were they, anyhow?"

"The Sheriff and two Pinkerton men," he answered, gravely. "They have arrested Bob and Tom for the hold-up."

"Owen," I gasped, standing up so suddenly that the U. S. mail flew in all directions. "You don't believe they were the ones, do you?"

"Not for a minute," Owen answered, with conviction. "And I told them so, but it seems the men have bad records and the description fits them. 'A tall man, with a Southern accent, and a short, slight, smaller man.' So they arrested them." Owen sat down. "It's absurd. In the first place,

they couldn't have gotten to the railroad in
time to hold up the limited. They didn't
leave here until nine o'clock, and in the next
place, they went home."

"But they didn't." I felt suddenly weak
in my knees. "I took the clothes over to
Mrs. Reed, and both she and Maggie were
wondering why they hadn't come."

Owen looked at me in blank amazement,
and then asked why on earth I hadn't told
him.

"Good heavens, Owen, I haven't seen you
a moment alone. And, besides, I never supposed it made any difference *where* the men
went. Hereafter if the angel Gabriel comes
to work for us, I shall insist upon knowing
where he spends his nights. Really," I
began to laugh, "you know, if we ever leave
this ranch, the only place we shall feel at
home is in the penitentiary. None but people with 'records' and 'pasts' will interest
us." I was half amused and wholly excited,
for even to have a speaking acquaintance
with the leading figures in a hold-up and
murder was something my wildest flight of

imagination could have scarcely pictured a few months before. Owen was really serious.

"Well, I must say," he shook his head and looked down at the floor, "it begins to look as though Bob and Tom might have some trouble proving they weren't the men. It's serious for them, since they weren't at home. The description certainly fits them." Owen took up the paper. " 'One man about five feet eight inches high, slender and light mustache, wearing old clothes and a rusty black slouch hat. The other man five feet ten inches tall, slender, short, black mustache, about forty years old, spoke with a Southern accent, wore an old black suit and an old striped rubber coat.' "

"Go on," I said, as Owen started to put the paper down; "I want to hear it." He read on:

" 'The men were supposed to have boarded the train coming from Denver, at a small station this side of Star. The Pullmans were on the rear. When the train stopped at the station, the Pullman conductor went out on the back platform and saw two men crouching in the vestibule. He told them to get off, but at that moment the train started, and they rose up, covering him with their revolvers. One got behind him, holding his gun against him, the other in front. They handed him a gunny-sack and made him carry it. In this manner they entered the body of the car.

" 'In the first car they got very little plunder, and pushed on into the next. As they entered the second sleeper, they met the porter, who was forced to elevate his hands and precede them. While they were engaged in robbing the passengers in the second Pullman, the train conductor entered, and was compelled to elevate his hands, with the rest.

" 'They paused at one berth and seemed very much incensed that the woman it contained was so slow in handing over her valuables. They swore and were very impatient. Suddenly, a man in the next berth thrust his head out between the curtains. He had a revolver in his hand and fired, but instantly another shot rang out from the robber in the rear, and the man sank back in his berth.

"'After the shooting, the robbers appeared more nervous and hurried. When they had gone through the car, they took the gunny-sack and emptied the contents into their pockets. One of the robbers pulled the bell-rope, but evidently not hard enough, for the train continued on its way. Swearing, they compelled the porter and two conductors to stand out on the platform with them, covered by their revolvers, until the train slowed down at Paxton, when they swung off to the ground and disappeared into these vast prairie lands, which are so sparsely settled one can drive for a day without seeing a person.

"'As soon as the train stopped, the passengers hurried to the berth of the man who had been shot, but he had been instantly killed.

"'The Sheriff was notified, and a posse started in pursuit, but the robbers had vanished.'"

Owen put down the paper, and we sat up far into the night talking it over.

Subsequently our ranch, our horses, and Owen's opinions were freely quoted in the press. Bob and Tom were positively identified by the three trainmen as the hold-ups. They were retained a week in jail, and then suddenly released on "insufficient proof."

Owen did not believe in point of time they could have held up the train, for he had talked to Bob that Saturday night until after nine o'clock, but everybody, including Owen, held them capable of it. The point was simply that they had not happened to be there.

Later Bob and Tom returned to the ranch, incensed at their arrest and detention, but no one ever learned where they were that memorable Saturday night.

Moreover, the men who held up the train were never found, and again one of those strange tragedies of the West ended in vagueness.

I was struck by the repetition of that

phenomenon "A crime, a tragedy." At first indignation and an earnest attempt to find the offenders and bring them to justice, then delay, and the whole affair shoved into the background by something newer.

Life here seemed to flow by like a stream at flood-tide. Who could stem that current long enough to catch those bits of human frailty floating on the surface, or follow them down stream to the sea?

V

A GOVERNMENT CONTRACT

FROM the first, I had been conscious of a fascination about the West impossible to describe. Its charm was too enigmatical and elusive for definition.

There was a suggestion of the sea in that vast circle and in the long, undulations of the prairie, as though great waves had become solidified, then clothed in softest green. No sign of restless movement was apparent in those billows which stretched away from the mountains into the vague distance. All was still. The towering mountain itself was the symbol of infinite peace and rest. Yet there, in the midst of that unbroken serenity, stood a cluster of buildings, the center of the greatest activity, where life was vital and thrilling as though a few human beings had been flung through space and dropped onto those silent plains to work out the age-long fight for existence.

Peace and conflict, silence and sound, absence of life and life in its most complex form; contrasts—everywhere and in everything—it could be defined, it was in "contrasts" that the fascination of the West was expressed.

Ranch life might be difficult; it was never commonplace. The mere sight of a lone horseman on a distant hill suggested greater possibilities of excitement than a multitude of people in a city street.

Each day brought so many new experiences, some of comedy, some of tragedy, that I began to look for them.

After the Government had awarded a contract to furnish "150 horses of a dark bay color for cavalry use" our life became dramatic, with the riders cast in the leading rôles.

The stage-setting consisted of a large circular corral, twelve feet high, built of heavy pitch-pine posts and three-inch planks with a massive snubbing post set in the center. Since there was "standing room only," cracks were at a premium.

The dramatis personae were two tall, slender-waisted cow-punchers who walked with a slightly rolling gait, due to extremely high-heeled boots, much too small for them. In their right hands they carried a coiled rope swinging easily. Their costumes were composed of cloth or corduroy trousers, dark-colored shirts, nondescript vests of some sort, dark blue or red handkerchiefs knotted loosely about their necks, expensively-made boots, the tops of which were covered by the legs of their "pants"; spurs, of course; high-priced Stetson hats, the crowns creased to a peak, and frequently encircled by the skin of a rattle-snake, and exceedingly soft gauntlet-gloves. It was my observation that the old-time cow-puncher wore gloves at all times. He did remove them when eating, and, I presume, before going to bed, but they were always in evidence.

The "Star" is a frightened, snorting "broncho," or unbroken horse which for the five or six years of its life had been running loose. Now it was to be "busted." It is cut out from the bunch and run into the corral and the gate securely fastened.

One of the men stands near the post, the other does the roping. Facing the men, the broncho stands still, his head high, his eyes wild and full of fear. An abrupt motion by one of the riders starts him on a frantic run around and around in a circle. A sudden throw of the rope and both front feet are in the loop. Quick as lightning the man settles back on it, both front legs are pulled out from under the horse and he falls on his side; the helper runs to his head, seizes the muzzle and twists it straight up, thrusts one knee against the neck and holds the top of the head to the ground. The roper puts two or three more loops above the front hoofs, passes the rope, now doubled forming a loop, between the legs, to one of the hind feet, then pulls on the end that he has all the time held. This action draws all three feet together. One or two more loops about them, a hitch and the horse is tied so that it is impossible for him to get up. While the

© By Permission W. G. Walker

INSPECTING A BRAND

broncho lies helpless, the saddle and bridle are put on, a large handkerchief passed under the straps of the bridle over the eyes and made fast. The rope is taken off. Feeling a measure of freedom, he staggers to his feet and stands. The cinches are drawn very tight, the rider mounts, gives a sharp order to "let him go," the man on the ground pulls the handkerchief from the eyes of the horse, and jumps aside.

For a moment the broncho stands dazed, then jumps, throws his head between his front legs almost to the ground, squeals, humps his back and pitches around and around the corral in a vain attempt to rid himself of the fearsome thing on his back. The circular corral, limited in space, gives little opportunity to succeed; the rider has the advantage. The horse stops pitching and runs frantically about the corral, at length tiring himself out. Dripping with sweat, trembling from fear and excitement, he comes to a slow trot. The gate is thrown open. Making a dash for freedom, he plunges through the outside corrals, the horseman or "circler" close beside him, trying to keep between the half-crazed broncho and any object he might run into. The horse bolts out into the open; his is the advantage now, and he makes the rider ride. He bucks this way and that, twisting, turning, jumping and running, the man on his back so racked and shaken it seems incredible that his body can hold together. They tear out over the prairie in a wild race, far off over the hills, out of sight now. After a time they come back on a walk. The broncho has been busted—the act has ended.

Should the horse rear and throw himself backward, there is the greatest danger that the man may be caught under him and killed, it happens so quickly, but these quiet, diffident chaps are absolutely fearless, past masters in the art of riding, facing death each time they ride a new horse, but facing it with the supreme courage of the commonplace, sitting calmly in the saddle, racked, shaken, jolted until at times the blood streams from their nose, yet after a short rest the rider "took up the next one" quite as though nothing at all had happened.

All the horses had to be broken and then made ready for the inspection of the Government officials, and the boys were working with them early and late.

It was an unusual experience to live in daily association with these men, in whom were combined characteristics of the Knights of the Round Table and those peculiar to the followers of Jesse James.

In Douglas, Wyoming, there stands a monument erected by the friends of a local character who, curiously, bore the same surname as the famous explorer for whom Pike's Peak was named. Chisled out of the solid granite these opposing traits are epitomized in this unique epitaph:

"Underneath this stone in eternal rest
  Sleeps the wildest one of the wayward west;
  He was gambler and sport and cowboy, too,
  And he led the pace in an outlaw crew;
  He was sure on the trigger and staid to the end,
  But he was never known to quit on a friend;
  In the relations of death all mankind is alike,
  But in life there was only one George W. Pike."

Strange, contrasting personalities—in awe of nobody, quite as ready to converse famil-

iarly with the President as with Owen, but
probably preferring Owen because they
knew he was a fine horseman.

Persons and things outside their own
world held but slight interest for them. At
first I had a hazy idea that I might be the
medium through which a glimpse of the outside world would broaden the narrow limits
of their lives. I planned to get books for
them and to arrange a reading room, but my
dream was soon shattered upon discovering
that this broader view possessed no charm.
Indeed, when I offered to teach Joe to read
he refused my offer without a moment's
hesitation, firmly announcing "I ain't goin'
to learn to read, 'cause then I'd have to!"
"Why, Mrs. Brook," he added, looking with
scorn at the book I held in my hand, "I
wouldn't be bothered the way you are for
nothin', havin' to read all them books in
there," nodding his head in the direction of
our cherished library. This was certainly a
fresh point of view regarding education.
About the same time I found that the Sears
and Roebuck or Montgomery Ward catalogue

might be fittingly called the Bible of the plains. Night after night the boys pored over them absorbed in the illustrations, of hats, gloves, boots and saddles, the things most dear to their hearts, for on their riding equipment alone they spent a small fortune.

Improvident and generous, however great their vices might be, their lives were free from petty meanness; the prairies had seemed to

> "Give them their own deep breadth of view
> The largeness of the cloudless blue."

The religion of the cow-puncher? My impression was that he had none, for certainly he subscribed to no conventional creed or dogma. Yet what was it that gave him a code of honor which made cheating or a lie an unforgivable offense and a man guilty of either an outcast scorned by his associates, and what was it that would have made him go without bread or shelter that a woman or child might not suffer?

Rough and gentle, brutal and tender, good and bad, not angel at one time and devil at another, but rather saint and sinner at the same time. Little of religious influence came into his life, and as for Bibles—there were none.

I remember the story of a Bishop who was travelling through the West and was asked to hold service in one of the larger towns. When he arrived he found that he had left his own Bible on the train, so he sent the hotel clerk out to borrow one. After some time the man returned with a Bible, explaining to the Bishop that it was the only one in town. "I went everywhere and finally got this one. It's the one they use at the Court House to swear on!"

The cow-puncher, however, could swear without any assistance, for usually "cussin'" formed a very necessary part of his conversation. But as I sat at my window sewing one summer morning I heard a violent argument at the corral between Fred and a new "hay-hand" from Kansas. Fred's voice was decisive.

"That's all right, but you cut out that cussin' here—the Missus' window's open, and she'll hear you." And the heart of "the Missus" warmed to her Knight of the Corral.

There was another incident, the true significance of which I did not know until three years after it occurred, when the foreman of the L— ranch met Owen in Denver and inquired for me, adding:

"Well, I'll never forget Mrs. Brook. Do you remember the day we was shippin' them white faces from the Junction about three years ago, when you and Mrs. Brook happened to come along and stopped to watch us? Well, one of the best men I had was brandin' a calf when it kicked him and he swore at it proper; all of a sudden he looked up and saw Mrs. Brook and another lady standin' on that high platform by the yards watchin' us. He was so plumb beat, he threw down his brandin' iron, took up his hat, walked across the street to a saloon and began drinkin' and stayed drunk for three days, and there I was, short-handed, with a train-load of cows and calves to ship."

Contrast again—chivalry carried to the

extent of being drunk for three days because he had sworn before a woman!

The horses were all being ridden and trained for the inspection which was soon to take place. Each man had his own "string," those he had broken, and every day they were put through their paces. When inspected, they had to be walked, trotted and run up and down before the officers, stopped instantly, and the veterinarian was supposed to put his ear to their chests to see if their breathing was regular and their hearts sound. Now, Western horses are not accustomed to having their hearts tested, and I noticed that while the riders did everything else that was required, they tacitly agreed "to let the vet do his own listnin'."

The day that the Army officers were to arrive, as Owen was getting ready to drive over to the station to meet them, I remarked casually that I hoped nothing would happen to upset their peace of mind, as it was very important that the honorable representatives of the Government be kept in a good humor. The house was still in an unsettled condition but for the time being it had been brought into sufficient order to insure their comfort. The larder was stocked with the best the markets afforded and the horses were being "gentled" daily.

When guests came on the train our dinner might be served at any hour up to ten o'clock at night for after their arrival at the station there was the sixteen mile drive to the ranch—and anything might happen. It was late that particular night when I heard them at the meadow gate. I couldn't understand why they stopped so long. There were sounds of confusion and as they entered the house one of the officers held up a finger dripping with blood, the Colonel's hat was awry, his clothes covered with mud, and they all appeared agitated and excited. I could not imagine what had happened. Then they all began to tell me at once.

Upon reaching the meadow gate the Lieutenant who acted as bookkeeper jumped out to open it but failed to return after they had driven through. Upon investigation they found he had caught his finger between the wire loop and the post and was held fast. They extricated him from his dilemma and drove on. It was very dark and upon reaching the house as the august Colonel descended from the wagon, he tripped over a pile of stones lying near the gate, fell down and just escaped breaking his neck. I tried to smile and yet be sympathetic—but I had a vision of Owen with "one hundred fifty horses of a dark bay color" on his hands if the good humor of the officers was not restored before morning.

They were shown to their rooms and I prayed nothing would happen to the Veterinarian, who had so far remained intact.

The Colonel and the Lieutenant had come down stairs. We were all in the library waiting for the Doctor before going in to dinner, when we heard a fearful crash. We rushed into the hall to see the poor man sitting on the steps holding both hands to his head. He was very tall and, coming down the narrow winding stairs, had struck his head on an overhanging projection which he had failed to observe. His injury was more uncomfortable than serious and had quite a cheering effect on his two companions, who began to chaff him about "taking off an inch or two" so by the time dinner was over they were all in high spirits.

The following morning at nine the inspection began. Each horse was brought out, looked over and measured to see that he came up to the stipulated number of "hands". If he passed he was immediately ridden.

Each of the men rode the horses he had broken. First the horse was walked up and down between the blacksmith-shop and the corral, then trotted and then run, after which his lungs and breathing were tested and if satisfactory he was accepted.

Every time a man got on to ride, I was conscious of a feeling of great uncertainty. The horses looked quiet enough and were fairly gentle, but Owen and I knew that the slightest variation in the manner of mounting or "touching them up" might cause them to go through a few movements not required by the United States Government.

As it was, all those we had expected to buck behaved like lambs, while those which had been considered fairly well broken did everything from bucking to snorting and blowing foam all over the Veterinarian when he attempted to examine their teeth and test their lungs.

For three days the inspection went on, each day more interesting than the last, until all the horses had been examined and out of the number the necessary one hundred and fifty accepted and branded U. S.

As the bunch of horses headed for Denver was being driven off the ranch, Fred looked after them reffectively—

"If them sodjers can ride, it'll be all right," he remarked, "but if they go to puttin' tenderfeet on them bronchs, they'll land in Kingdom-come before they ever hit the saddle."

VI

A VARIETY OF RUNAWAYS

L IFE in any primitive, sparsely settled country is fraught with adventure. It is the element which gives zest to everyday affairs and which lifts existence above the commonplace, but since everything has its price, the price of untrammelled living must often be paid in discomfort and inconvenience.

To us, and to many others, abounding health and freedom were ample compensations for a few annoying circumstances but with our guests it was a more serious consideration. After a few experiences we began to discourage the visits of those unfitted by nature and temperament for "roughing it".

We could not control the elements nor untoward events. Fate had such an invariable custom of upsetting and rearranging all of our most carefully laid plans that when friends, especially "tenderfeet", arrived, we had a premonition that before they departed something would happen. It never failed.

In the house our guests were exempt from anxiety and discomfort, but no one cared to stay indoors when a dazzling world of blue, green and gold lay just outside, and the unexpected was no regarder of persons. A cloud-burst was just as apt to descend upon the unsuspecting head of a delicate, carefully nurtured old lady as was an indiscriminating rattlesnake to frighten some timid soul into hysterics.

Everyone who came to the ranch wanted to ride, those knowing least about horses being the most insistent, and not wishing to take any chances, at first we gave them Billy, gentle, trustworthy Billy, who, when running loose, could be caught by a man on foot and ridden into the corral with a handkerchief around his neck instead of a bridle. We would start out, the tenderfoot joyously "off for a horseback ride," and the next thing we knew he would be off the horse doubled up under a fence or lying flat on the prairie, while Billy peacefully nibbled grass. No one could explain it unless the uninitiated had lost a stirrup and had unwittingly given the horse a dig in the ribs which was immediately resented—so even Billy was disqualified.

The truth was, none of our horses was sufficiently well broken for the inexperienced horseman to ride or drive. They behaved very decently until something occurred, which was out of the ordinary, and then the reaction was most sudden and disastrous.

With the stock on the ranch we had acquired about four hundred horses, most of which had never been handled and were running loose on the range. Before they were of any use or value they had to be broken and Owen felt that it was one of the most important things to be done. Consequently, many of the horses were broken to drive in the hay field, the broncho hitched up with a gentle horse, and put onto the rake or mowing machine—many were the runaways.

Charley was leisurely by nature. He never

hurried either in speech or movement. Owen and I were in the office one morning when he strolled around the house and up to the door.

"Mis-ter Brook," he drawled, "Ja-ne and Maud are running away with the mow-ing machine down in the timber— they throw-ed Windy off the seat," but before he got the last word out, his listener was down the steps, over the fence and on his way toward the creek where Maud and Jane were tearing through the timber leaving parts of the mowing machine on stumps and fallen logs, while Charley looked after him in mild surprise. The horses were brought to an abrupt stop when one tried to go on one side of a tree and the other on the opposite side.

There was a beautiful black horse, "Toledo", that refused to allow anyone to come near him but Owen or Bill, and there was also a new man on the ranch who so constantly boasted of his ability to handle bronchos the boys had dubbed him "Windy".

Windy concluded one day that he would harness Toledo alone. There were violent sounds in the stable, snorts, shouts, thumps, and Windy sailed through the open door and landed on a conveniently placed pile of manure, frightened to death but unhurt.

Bill was furious.

"What'd you do to him, anyhow?" he stormed after roping Toledo who had broken his halter and was running loose in the corral.

"I didn't do nothin' to him," protested Windy. "I just crope up and retched over and tetched him and he begun to snort and cave 'round."

"Course you didn't do nothin', you couldn't do nothin' if you tried. You'd better go back to town where you belong, 'stead a stayin' out here spoilin' good horses." Bill's choler was rising. "You don't know nothin' neither, you're jest a bone head, your spine's jest growed up and haired over." And, leading the subdued Toledo, Bill disappeared into the stable.

When the team that Owen reserved for his own use had passed the kicking and lunging stage and I had become sufficiently confident to look at the landscape instead of watching their ears, he usually concluded they were "pretty well broken" and that he must try out a new one. This trying out process went on indefinitely, for Owen's New England conscience gave him no peace apparently while an unbroken horse remained in his possession. It was a form of duty.

When we had guests we used, what my husband was pleased to call, a gentle team, one that started off decorously with all their feet on the ground instead of in the air, but one day when we were expecting some friends from Wyoming he could not resist driving a new pair of beautiful bay horses when we went to meet them. I remained behind.

The dinner hour passed and no Owen; additional hours went by and late at night he came in dusty, dirty and scratched.

In response to a perfect volley of questions he explained that he was all right, but the Lawtons had telegraphed they had been detained, and then he added, as quite an unimportant detail, that "the horses had run away". He had the expression of a fond and indulgent parent, and as he did not rise to the defense of his pet team when I called them "miserable brutes" I knew his pride, at least, had suffered.

"You see," he resumed, "your new sewing machine and some other freight was at the station, so when I found the Lawtons were not coming I thought I'd bring it over. I had the crystal clock, too." Owen looked so sheepish I had to laugh, although the clock had been a wedding present which we had sent up to the jeweler to be regulated.

"Is it smashed?"

"Oh, no," he reassured me, "but I don't know how well it will run. I got out to close the gate beyond the railroad when a confounded freight engine whistled and the horses started. I was holding the reins in my hand, of course, and tried to climb in the back of the wagon, but couldn't make it on account of the load. I ran along the side until the horses went so fast I fell down and when they began to drag me I let go of the reins. They ran all over that inclosure, the wagon upset and canned tomatoes, sewing machine and crystal clock were strewn everywhere. I caught the horses finally, but the wagon was smashed so I had to walk back to Becker's, get his wagon and pick up all the freight—that's what delayed me. I'm dreadfully sorry about the sewing machine and the clock, but I don't believe they are much hurt."

He was very contrite, was my husband, but it didn't last long, that sense of duty was too insistent. A very short time after, he was alone, driving another team, with a horse he had just bought, tied to the tug. The new horse, frightened at a dead animal in the lane, jumped, broke the tug, plunged forward, pulled the neck yoke off, the buggy tongue stuck into the ground as the horses ran, the buggy heaved up in the air and pitched Owen out. He landed so close to a fence post his head was scratched, but he might have been killed. As long as he had escaped, this runaway had its amusing side, too. He was bringing home a quantity of china nest-eggs which followed when he was thrown out, and he said for a minute it fairly snowed nest-eggs; the ground was white with them.

Owen and his horses! I never could decide whether it was more nerve-racking to go with him or stay behind, so I usually took the chance and went. The experiences we had! I wonder we ever survived that horse-breaking period, but only once did we face a fate from which there seemed only one chance in a thousand of escaping with our lives.

We were driving a buckskin horse Owen had just bought and a newly broken mare, a handsome, high spirited creature called Beauty. She danced and she pranced and forged ahead of the new horse which became nervous and excited in trying to keep up with her.

We were going up a long hill. Beauty was pulling and tugging on the bit when suddenly she gave a toss to her head and to our horror we saw the bridle fall back around her neck. The bit had broken. Like a flash she was off, the other horse running with her. Owen spoke to them. He wound the reins about his arms and pulled on them with all his strength.

At the top of the hill there was a fairly level space where Owen tried to circle them, hoping to tire them out, but he had no control over Beauty and she wheeled about starting back over the road we had come, the buggy bouncing and swaying behind. There was a fence corner with an old post standing about ten feet from it. The horses headed straight for it. I closed my eyes, expecting that we would be wrecked, but they turned and raced across a gulch, the buggy lurched, tipped, struck one side and then the other, but by a miracle did not upset.

I saw that Owen was trying to head them into a fence and braced myself for the shock, realizing that he hoped to entangle them in the barbed wire and so throw them, but just as we reached it Beauty veered to one side almost overturning the buggy. We were so close the skirt of Owen's fur coat caught on the barbs and was instantly torn to ribbons and we heard the vibrating "ping" of the wire along its entire length as the wheels struck the fence.

© By Permission R. R. Doubleday

THE "STAR" IS A FRIGHTENED, SNORTING "BRONCHO"

On and on the maddened horses raced, up hills, down long slopes, through gulches in which it seemed we must be wrecked, until at length we reached the crest of a hill at the bottom of which, angling with the fence, ran a deep gulch with high cut banks. We knew that if the frantic horses reached the edge of that bank at the rate we were going there was no escape for us and we should plunge over the embankment with the horses. To jump was impossible. I was in despair, realizing that Owen, pulling on the horses with all his might, was nearly exhausted.

"Owen, isn't there something I can do?" It was the first time a word had been spoken.

"Pull on the Buckskin," he answered quickly.

I leaned forward and seized the rein with both hands as far down as I could reach and threw myself back with all my weight. The Buckskin was pulled back on his haunches, Beauty stopped. Owen handed me the reins, another moment he was at their heads calling to me to jump. In that instant before jumping I lived an eternity, for if the horses had started again I should have gone to certain death alone.

I was so weak with fright and sudden relief when I felt the firm earth under my feet I could scarcely stand but I had to get to the Buckskin's head and hold on to him, for Owen had his hands full with Beauty, who began to rear and plunge. It was no time for nerves. The horses were finally unhitched. Owen led Beauty and I, the Buckskin. Leaving the buggy on the edge of that yawning gulch, we walked the five miles back to the ranch.

VII

THE MEASURE OF A MAN

THE Bohms had gone. The last load of furniture, upon which old Bohm perched like an ill-omened bird, had disappeared through the gate on the top of the hill. At last, after six months of vexation and trouble, Owen and I could live our own life and run the ranch without interference.

Bohm had tried to wriggle out of every clause in his contract. He had delayed gathering and turning over the stock by every means and had invented a thousand excuses for staying on from week to week. It had made it very difficult and had exasperated Owen. If he hadn't been wise and patient beyond words, Bohm's bones long before would have mingled with those of his reputed victims in the old root cellar. I had a different end planned for him each day, but

none seemed really fitting. Owen had gone
on in his own way, however, insisting upon
every part of the contract being fulfilled and
reducing Bohm to impotent rage by his quiet
firmness.

Mrs. Bohm had recovered from her "fainting spells" and her husband was furious to
think he had sold the ranch. In desperation
he finally sent to San Francisco for his
brother, who was a lawyer, to see if there
was any possibility of getting out of the contract. The "Judge" was a nice old chap, who
looked like an amiable Mormon with a long
beard. He soon settled the question.

"Why, Jim, you wanted to sell out, you
signed the contract and you have your
money. You'll have to stay with your bar-
gain now, whether you like it or not."

We always remembered him kindly for this
and for a story he told. We had been discussing the Chinese as servants and he said:

"Well, I had one for two years, but I don't
want any more. I want to know what I'm
eating and with those heathen you are never
sure.

"It had been raining very hard one day when Wong came to me in the afternoon and said:

" 'Judge, him laining outside, me gottee no meat for dinner.'

"I told him that we would do without meat for it was raining too hard for anyone to go out who didn't have to. Wong looked dejected for he liked meat. He turned to go out of the room, when his eyes fell on the cat. His face brightened with a sudden inspiration.

" 'Have meat for dinner! Kill'em cat!'

"Kill the cat! What on earth do you mean?

" 'Less, kill'em cat,' he repeated in a matter of fact tone, 'him sick anyhow.' "

We had asked the Bohms to take their meals with us, but only Mrs. Bohm came to our table. Bohm preferred to eat with the men. We suspected that he was trying to cause trouble. Charley unconsciously confirmed our suspicions. He was always conversational and seized the opportunity to talk while fixing my window screen.

"Say, Mrs. Brook, you'd orter seen Bill this mornin'. He was eatin' flapjacks to beat time and was just reachin' for more, when old Bohm, with that mean way of his, began slammin' Mr. Brook. He was sayin' you folks thought you was too good to eat in the kitchen with us common fellers and had to have a separate dinin' room, when Bill just riz up out of his chair so sudden it went over backwards, and believe me, his eyes had sparks in 'em when he came back at the old man.

" 'Tain't that the Brooks think that they're too good, but there's some folks too stinkin' common for anybody to eat with'—and out of the door he walked and all the boys follered him, leavin' Bohm alone there facin' all them flapjacks. I reckon he'd a rather faced them flapjacks than Bill, though,—Gee, Bill was some hot," and Charley's blue eyes sparkled at the reminiscence.

It was exactly as I thought; the boys despised Bohm and were absolutely loyal to Owen.

After this episode, Owen had a long talk with Bill and a short, heated interview with

Bohm, which resulted in the old man's reluctant, but hasty, departure.

I drew a long breath of relief when I saw the last wagon disappear and looked up fully expecting to see the dove of peace pluming herself on our roof-tree. But apparently doves in the cattle country never alight,— they just pass by.

Owen had bought several thousand acres of land from the railroad. A car of barbed wire for the fence, which was to encircle the entire ranch, was at the station. Our land was now in one solid block with the exception of a few acres of Government land which could only be acquired by homestead entry. This limited acreage in the great checkerboard was all that remained of the "free range."

At this juncture Owen was served with a notice by the United States Marshal forbidding him to build the fence. It would enclose Government land. Every mile of the proposed fence would have been on ground which he had bought, paid for, and on which he was paying taxes—but still—he could not fence

it. "Government land must remain unin-
closed." It made no difference, apparently,
what happened to the cattleman whose
money was tied up in property he could not
use. Government land must remain free and
open to the public. But, while those few
acres of free range remained open to the
public, thousands of acres of our unprotected
land remained open also. Everyone used it.
The ranchmen for miles around, learning
that Owen was forbidden to fence, gathered
all their cattle and threw them onto our land.

It was a very serious problem. Our range
was being destroyed, the grass was eaten off
so closely nothing remained for winter range.
Our full-blooded Hereford breeding stock was
of little use to us. All our money was in-
vested in land and cattle and there was only
one thing left to do,—put riders on our range
to drive the other cattle off.

Upon this solution of the problem the dove
of peace promptly departed and we entered
upon a long, hard struggle for the possession
and use of what was our own. Owen was
faced, not only with financial failure, but ab-

solute ruin. The future was far from bright, but when an old school-mate came with her husband to visit us it seemed positively brilliant by contrast.

Alice Joice and I had been devoted friends for years. The summer before we had spent in Europe, where I had left her, deep in the study of Art, to which she intended "to devote" her life.

"It is so commonplace to marry, Esther," these were her parting words; "any woman can marry—but so few can have a real career."

Alice's "career" had abruptly ended in "commonplace matrimony," for she had just married a Mr. Van Winkle from Brooklyn, a man I had never met. They were touring the West and were most anxious to include our ranch. I was very eager to see them so I wrote, urging her to come, but asked her to let us know when to expect them, so there would be no mistake about our being at the station.

I was particularly anxious to have them see ranch life at its best for they were our first guests. The house looked very attractive with all our own furniture and wedding presents in place, but I thought the guest room floor might be improved so I painted it Saturday afternoon. Then everything went wrong: the wind-mill pump failed to work, the whole pipe had to be pulled out of the well; we were without running water in the house and couldn't have a fire in the kitchen range, so rations were extremely light.

Supper, consisting chiefly of sardines, awaited Owen, who was trying to get some of the grease off his hands, when a homesteader by the name of Hamm, his wife, sister and five children drove up. He had come to see Owen on business and they were invited in to supper.

The table was lengthened and reset, more sardines were opened and we were just ready to sit down when my Aunt, who was standing near the window, exclaimed:

"Who on earth is that!"

Who, indeed! Alice Joice and her husband with a team they had hired at the station.

Having a strong heart I did not faint, but left Auntie to help the maid make the necessary additions to the table—and sardines, while Owen and I hurried out to greet them.

"Hello, dearie, here we are," Alice called from the wagon as I approached. "Clarence and I thought it would be such fun to surprise you. How-do-you-do, Mr. Brook, I want you to meet my husband, Mr. Van Winkle." Alice jumped off the step and threw herself into my arms. "Oh, Esther, isn't this fun?" Gay, inconsequent Alice, from her city home, never considered for a moment that a surprise *could* be anything but joyous.

If I had met him in Egypt, I should have known that her husband's name was Van Winkle—Clarence Van Winkle, it couldn't have been anything else.

He was pale and tall and thin and rigid. The inflexibility of the combined ancestral spines had united in his back bone. He might break, he could never bend. My imagination failed when I tried to picture the meeting between the heir to the Van Winkle name and the Hamms. It was far worse than anything I could ever have imagined.

Alice was very sweet; she talked all the time, patted the five little Hamms and won their mother's heart by asking their names and ages, but in acknowledging the introduction Clarence only bowed slightly, a movement which required great effort, then relapsed into silence immediately, scrutinizing the Hamm family through his glasses as though they were rare animals in a Zoo. Mrs. Hamm and her sister were stupefied and did not speak a word, but Mr. Hamm, a truly sociable person from Oklahoma, continually addressed Clarence as "young feller," which produced the same effect as a violent chill, and when he joyously jogged a Van Winkle elbow to emphasize some pleasantry, Clarence firmly moved his chair out of reach of the defiling touch.

Alice ate everything and did not stop talking for a moment. Clarence refused everything but a cracker, which he munched in silence. Suddenly he turned white and left the table. Owen escorted him out-of-doors while Alice and I followed. He was faint, just faint, and collapsed weakly onto a garden seat. Alice said it was the Denver water, but I suspected unassimilated Hamm. Owen stayed with him and Alice and I returned to finish supper. The Hamms left soon after and Clarence gradually revived under the influence of Owen's New England accent and Scotch whisky.

All at once I thought of the freshly painted guest-room floor. I explained the situation to Alice and we went up to see if it was dry. It was, but the smell of paint was most evident. Alice gave a few sniffs and said apologetically:

"I'm dreadfully sorry, Esther, but Clarence couldn't possibly sleep here. He is so sensitive to odors of any kind." I was reminded of a faint aroma which had clung to the Hamm garments. "If there is another room we can occupy, I think it would be better." Alice was accustomed to hotels. I offered our room; it was reluctantly but finally accepted, the scion of the Van Winkles must not breathe paint. All the things from the guest-room were put in our room and ours were moved up to the guest-room.

Just before they retired Alice confided to me that Clarence had had some temperature in Denver and the Doctor thought he might be threatened with typhoid fever.

"I really believe, Esther, if Clarence has any temperature in the morning we had better go back to Denver."

I reassured her as I bade her good-night and then sought Owen. I was beginning to have some temperature myself.

"Owen, if Clarence Van Winkle has a thousandth of a degree of temperature in the morning don't tell him that he'll be all right; let him go back to Denver or anywhere else he pleases. Imagine that man with typhoid, here."

The next morning Alice appeared at breakfast alone. Clarence had no temperature, but he felt weak and thought he had better stay in bed. He continued to feel weak for three days, Alice dancing attendance while the rest of us tried to get the household and water running again.

When Clarence finally emerged from his

seclusion, he was in high spirits, positively buoyant.

"Well, now I want to see everything, all the cattle, the cow-boys, branding, dehorning, a round-up and what is it you call it? Oh, yes, 'broncho busting'. We have to go back to Denver tomorrow, you know." He had to stop for want of breath.

Alice beamed fondly upon her enthusiastic bridegroom. Mine looked far from enthusiastic. Owen was a perfect host but he could not give a demonstration of a year's work in one day. The horse-breaking was over for the season and the branded and dehorned cattle scattered over miles of country. This he endeavored to explain to Clarence who made no attempt to conceal his disappointment nor his petulance.

"Oh, how unfortunate. I've heard so much of the fascination of ranch life I thought I'd like to see a little of it. I thought you had broncho busting or something interesting or entertaining going on every day."

Owen bit his lip. He was busy beyond words but he dropped everything and that afternoon we took our guests for a drive over the ranch. The wagon was new and rattled and, wishing to spare Clarence's delicate sensibilities, Owen put on some washers.

We were in the middle of the prairie miles from the house, Clarence had recovered his good humor since he was "actually seeing something", as he tactfully expressed it, when one of the wheels began to drag. The washers proved to be too tight, we had a hot spindle. There was nothing to do but sit there in the blazing sun while the two men took off the wheel, removed a washer or two and greased the spindle.

I wouldn't have missed it, the mere thought of that scene was a joy to me for months afterwards. Clarence Van Winkle red and perspiring from the effort of lifting a wheel, wiping his greasy hands on a piece of dirty waste! Alice's face was a study. I had to keep my eyes fixed on the landscape after one look over the side of the wagon. I was afraid I should laugh out loud.

The day they left Bill drove us all to the station. We just made the train, which was standing on the track as we arrived. Owen hurried to check the Van Winkle's baggage. Bill had to stay with the horses. Alice and I had all the wraps, which left Clarence to carry two dress suit cases across the tracks. His eyes were fixed on the porter and he was hurrying toward the Pullman when he stubbed his toe on one rail, sprawled all the way across the track and hit his neck on the second rail. The suit cases flew in one direction, his hat in another, his glasses fell off and his watch dropped out of his pocket. Alice and I rushed to the rescue, the porter assisted Clarence to his feet and picked up the suit cases, we gathered up the rest of the articles while Clarence stood in the middle of the track rubbing his knees, to the great amusement of the passengers. Alice went up to him when suddenly he screwed his face up as a child does before it begins to cry, threw both arms around her neck and buried his face on her shoulder. The conductor terminated the scene by calling "All aboard". Clarence limped to the train, rubbing his neck, and the last we saw was Alice holding all the wraps, the hat, glasses and watch, waving to us from the vestibule and Clarence comfortably seated in the Pullman smiling a wan farewell through the window. As the train with its precious freight was lost to sight around a curve, Owen and I began to laugh. We laughed until we were so weak we could scarcely get into the wagon. Bill's face was perfectly serious, but his eyes had a little twinkle in them as he said with his slow drawl:

"Lord, Mrs. Brook, I'm glad that young man married that girl. He'd orter have somebody look after him. A poor little goslin' feller like that ain't got no business goin' round alone."

Bill always sized up a situation in the fewest possible words.

During the drive back to the ranch I thought of Alice and her future by the side of a man of that type. Our future was uncertain enough, but if trouble and vicissitudes were our portion, at least I had someone with whom to share them.

Tex had been away for several weeks and

we were surprised to see him at the gate as we drove up. He looked very serious as he asked Owen if he might speak with him and Owen looked more serious when he came out of the office after their conversation.

"What is it, Owen? Something is wrong. Please tell me."

Owen took me by the arm and we walked up and down under the trees.

"Tex came over to tell me, Esther, that I am to be arrested for 'driving cattle off the range.' Technically, it's a serious charge, carrying a heavy fine and—" he paused— "imprisonment, but don't worry, my dear," as he felt me start a little at his last words, "it's listed on the statute books as a criminal offence, connected with rustling, but that can't hold in this case. It's a 'frame-up' to give me trouble, that's all. It might have been serious but Tex heard of it and came to warn me just in time. There's been a plot to eat me out and now they want to drive me out. I'm going in to Denver to see my lawyer tomorrow. I'm more troubled on your account than anything else."

"Don't worry about me, Owen, we're going to stay in this country and fight it out to the end. I'll face anything, as long as you don't cry," and we went into the house laughing, as we thought of Clarence Van Winkle.

The miserable experience which followed was sufficiently serious, even after the charge had been changed to one of minor character.

Owen was arrested on our anniversary. I went his bond. There was a long, expensive law-suit which we lost, the Judge contending that if a man wished to protect his land he should fence it. It was explained that the Government had forbidden it, but the Judge said that did not affect the verdict in this case. Owen paid the damages awarded by the Court, we gathered together our sixteen cow-puncher witnesses who had been staying with us at one of the largest hotels in Denver, an event for the cow-punchers, and returned to the ranch.

Did Owen weep on my shoulder? He set his lips a little more firmly and his face had an added sternness as he looked across those miles of rolling prairie he owned but which now were utterly useless.

He broke the silence at last. His voice had a different tone.

"I am going to have the use of my own land. They shan't keep me out of it any longer. I am going to sell off all the cattle and put in sheep. Then we'll see! With herders we don't need fences and cattle won't graze where sheep have ranged."

Thus with the first year of our marriage, the first chapter of our ranch experience ended and a totally different life began.

VIII
THE SHEEP BUSINESS

WITH the coming of the sheep everything was changed. It was like living in a different age, almost as though we had slipped back hundreds of years into Biblical times and had come into intimate association with Jacob and Joseph. With the advent of the wool or lamb buyers there was a sudden transition to the more commercial atmosphere of the twentieth century, but it was so fleeting our pastoral existence was scarcely interrupted.

A few of our old men had gone, Tex among them. He left with regret, but as he said—

"Lord knows I hate to go, Mr. Brook, but cattle's all I know and an old cow man ain't got no business around sheep; they just naturally despise each other." And he went up into Montana where the cattle business still flourished.

Most of the other men stayed on, however, to ride the fence lines, look after the horses and do the various things about the ranch, but the days of branding, dehorning and round-ups were past and the cow-puncher was replaced by "camp tenders".

The sheep were trailed all the way from New Mexico. Steve, who spoke Spanish, was foreman, and with three of the other men on horseback had come up the trail with the sheep and the soft-voiced Mexican herders.

Their entire camp equipment was skillfully packed on diminutive burros. It was somewhat startling to see what appeared to be animated wood-piles, water-casks, rolls of bedding or dish-pans bobbing about over the woolly backs of the sheep, until a parting in the band revealed the legs and lowered head of a sleepy-eyed burro.

The herders spoke no English and it was so charming to receive a gleaming smile and low bow while being addressed as "Padron" and "Señora" that we plunged into the study of their musical language forthwith.

Each herder was in charge of a band of

from fifteen hundred to twenty-five hundred sheep. Two herders occupied a camp, but the sheep were placed in separate corrals and, in order to give the various bands ample pasturage, the camps were placed miles apart.

Early in the morning the sheep were driven out, the herders taking their bands in opposite directions. All day long the flock quietly grazed over the prairie, the Mexican with his dog at his feet standing like a sentinel on a hill from which he could overlook his entire band and ward off any prowling coyote whose approach was heralded by a sudden scurry among the sheep.

Eternal vigilance, faithfulness and good judgment were the essential qualities in a herder, judgment in the handling of the sheep, in the selection of the best grass and water, the time for taking them out and bringing them back to the camp. The herders were not supposed to meet and talk together for while they were engrossed in conversation or out of sight of the sheep the two bands might become mixed, a very serious thing when the ewes were accompanied by their lambs, for when the bands were separated again the lamb might be in one band and its mother in the other.

It was a lonely life, but one for which Mexicans are especially suited. They lack the initiative of the Anglo-Saxons, they are naturally tranquil, slow of speech and action and content to do nothing—gentle children from the land of Mañana.

Scattered over the prairie, the sheep from a distance looked like mere dots so closely resembling the clumps of weeds, it was necessary to locate the herder before they could be identified. He looked like a solitary fence post placed on the top of a hill.

The Mexicans were most gracious and responsive, so delighted to receive a visit from the Padron that it was a joy to talk with them. We were never certain just what we had said, to be sure, but the effect of our halting, broken sentences of Spanish appeared so pleasing, we were convinced that if we could only converse fluently our words would become immortal.

Urbanity was most contagious. Owen and I made deep bows to the herders, we almost bowed to the sheep in an over-mastering desire to equal the politeness of Ramon, Fidel, Francisco or Tranquilino. What names! The atmosphere of the ranch became so poetic and romantic I should not have been surprised to see Owen adopt long hair and a flowing tie. After a day spent in visiting the sheep camps I returned in an ecstatic mood. I almost fancied myself the reincarnated spirit of Bo-Peep or Ramona but alas, my true identity was always disclosed as soon as I reached the house — I was only "the Missus".

Nevertheless the sheep business was fascinating, and best of all successful. The question of the range was settled. We had the use of our own land and our rights were respected. The customary feud between the sheepman and the cattle owners was avoided, since our sheep were always kept within the limits of the land which we owned. From being the object of hatred and vilification, Owen became a personage; his opinion

TRAILED ALL THE WAY FROM NEW MEXICO

LIKE A SOLITARY FENCE POST

quoted, his method of handling sheep emulated.

There were a few sheep men in the country who had made an indifferent success. They had scoffed at Owen's practice of selling off all the lambs in the autumn and maintaining the number of his sheep by additional purchases but, when they found how small his losses were, they promptly adopted his plan and even some of the old-time cattle men put in sheep.

The loss of the law suit had certainly proved to be the turning point in the history of the Brook family. Our popularity increased so rapidly it was amusing. Bill expressed what I felt as I met him riding through the meadow.

"Have you been riding the fence lines, Bill?"

"Yes'm, but it's just takin' exercise for my health. There ain't nothin' wrong any more. Since you folks got the world by the tail and a down-hill pull, everybody's huntin' around seein' what they can do to make it pleasant for you. I notice the Three Circle outfit don't go round no more leavin' all the gates open and when we get a fence line staked out, the stakes ain't all pulled up by mornin'."

"It is peaceful, isn't it?"

"Peaceful," echoed Bill, with feeling, "I'm so chuck full of peace I can't hardly hold any more. I'll bet if a feller was to hit me, I'd only 'baa-a'."

There was a vast amount of "Baa-ing" going on at the ranch, where Mary and I were raising a few score orphan lambs on the bottle. There was a voracious chorus whenever we appeared. They jumped all over us and as soon as they got hold of the nipple of the bottle they flopped down on their knees and did not release it until they had gulped down the last drop of milk, after which they stood up, their little sides sticking out as though they had been stuffed. As much care had to be exercised with the bottles, the temperature and quantity of the milk as though we had been feeding so many babies.

There was no milk at the outside camps

and no one to care for the poor abandoned lambs whose frivolous young mothers refused to own them, leaving them to starve. Occasionally an old ewe of truly maternal instinct could be fooled into adopting one of these little "dogies" or "bums". The skin of her dead lamb was taken off and slipped over the orphan, which was joyfully accepted because of its smell!

When the lambs made their appearance in May, the bands were separated, we had additional herders and they had to be more watchful for "Spring lamb" is also very tempting to coyotes. It was easy for a herder to lose ten or twenty lambs, for the little things congregate behind rocks or clumps of weeds and go to sleep, are overlooked when the sheep are driven back to the camp in the evening, and become the victims of those prairie wolves which continually lurk about.

Sometimes when we were driving, a tiny white speck would come racing after the wagon, a lamb, which had been left behind. Lambs are such senseless little things, when they are frightened they will adopt any moving object in lieu of a mother.

We pulled them out of prairie-dog holes into which they had thrust their heads and become fastened by having the loose earth fall in about their necks—they were troublesome but so appealing and amusing, they were a never-ending source of entertainment from the first moment they appeared, a tiny body supported on long, wabbly legs.

As they grew stronger "playful as a lamb" acquired a new meaning. They capered and they bucked, they raced around the corral in the evening when the ewes were contentedly lying down, they frisked about on the backs of their patient mothers, they jumped stiff-legged, and in a wild excess of joy bounded into the air giving a cork-screw twist to their hindquarters, which produced a most ludicrous effect.

Old quotations from the Bible came to have added significance; as the shearer held a poor frightened sheep between his knees and rapidly clipped off the fleece with his gleaming shears, there was not a sound if a clumsy movement cut a deep gash in the tender flesh; the "sheep before her shearer was dumb" indeed.

I spent days in the shearing sheds watching the proceedings from a pile of wool sacks or passing out small metal disks in exchange for the fleeces the shearers turned in. At the end of the day the disks were counted and each shearer credited with the number of sheep he had shorn.

The fleeces were rolled and tied separately, then thrown up to a man on a platform, who packed them in a long sack which was suspended from the top of a high frame. As it was filled, it was taken down, sewed up and rolled into the end of the shed to remain until later in the season when the wool was sold and hauled to the railroad.

Life was certainly peaceful compared to what it had been, but there was little danger of our becoming "on weed", as a certain retired cattle-man expressed it after a short sojourn in Europe.

Lambing, shearing and dipping followed in rapid succession. The herders cooked for themselves and once a week the wagons were piled with supplies and provisions which were left at each camp. In a huge store-room were kept quantities of salt-pork, sugar, dried fruits, coffee, flour and other groceries. Flour was bought by the ton and everything else in proportion. Making out the orders, having all the freight hauled the sixteen miles from the railroad, checking it out and keeping the camps supplied, were only details but it was the multitude of detail which filled the days and kept us from becoming "on weed". We issued the supplies to the camp-tenders ourselves, after one of them had filled all of the Mexicans' cans with gasoline instead of coal-oil, because "it kind'a had the same smell."

Unless we chanced to have guests, for weeks at a time the only women I saw were those in our employ, but I resented having any of my friends think of my life as "dull" or "lonely". On the contrary it was fascinating, full of incident, rich in experience which money could not buy. Living so close to the great heart of nature during those years on the plains, the vision of life partook of their breadth and a new sense of values replaced old, artificial standards. To be alone on the vast prairie was to gain a new conception of infinity and—eternity.

The Mexicans stayed on the ranch about nine months, then returned to their homes for a short visit. They were the most invariable creatures I ever knew. When they departed for Taos or Trinidad or Antonito, perhaps in July, they would announce on what date and by what train they would return in October. That was the end of it, and upon the appointed day in October someone would meet the designated train from which the smiling herder alighted. They never failed and they never left until another herder was there to take care of the sheep.

One summer during this vacation period, eight new herders came to replace eight that were going home. They were a fierce looking lot from a different section of the country. They had been on the ranch only a short time when Steve began to have trouble with them. They were late getting their sheep out in the morning, they drove them too rapidly and brought them in too early in the evening. In a few weeks the sheep began to lose flesh and show the effects of bad handling.

The newcomers disobeyed all orders, unless Steve happened to be on the spot. He had to watch them constantly. He came up to a camp unexpectedly one noon and found two of these Mexicans ready to sit down to a dinner they had just cooked. It was an invariable rule that the herders should take a lunch with them, for their mid-day meal, and not return to the camp. They had left their sheep alone, so Steve made them leave their dinner and go back to their bands, while he stayed to make sure they did not return.

It was impossible to discharge them until new herders could be brought from New Mexico and he and Owen talked over the situation at length that night.

Early in the morning Steve went out on another trip of inspection. About two o'clock he rode into the yard, his face covered with blood from a deep gash in his head. He fell from his horse into Owen's arms. We brought him in, washed off the blood, gave him a stimulant and waited until he was able to tell us what had happened.

It developed that as he came in sight of the camp he saw four of the Mexicans outside of the cabin. They stood motionless as he approached, then began to hurl rocks at him. One hit his horse and he was nearly thrown but managed to keep his seat. He was struck several times on the body. Although realizing that the Mexicans intended to kill him, he jumped off his horse and went toward them. A rock struck his head, but with undaunted courage he picked up some of the rocks and threw them back at the herders. They had not expected that turn to the affair and ran into the cabin. Steve was unarmed and too badly hurt, single handed, to deal with the Mexicans, so he got on his horse, with difficulty, and came back to the ranch.

The next thing I knew, Owen, Bill and Fred, each carrying a gun, got into the wagon and drove off.

When anything happened it came with such suddenness there was never opportunity for questions, besides, my association with men had taught me the value of silence—in an emergency.

In a few hours Owen and Fred came back. They had met the eight new herders walking into the ranch to "quit". They walked back to their respective camps instead, their pace accelerated by a loaded gun pointing at their backs. The cabins were searched, several villainous looking knives confiscated and eight subdued cut-throats returned to the peaceful occupation of herding sheep, under Bill's watchful eye and loaded gun.

Owen said that it wasn't at all necessary for the Mexicans to understand English since Bill's few remarks were sufficiently lurid to attract their attention.

Until other herders could be brought to the ranch, one white man, always armed, stayed at each camp, constantly on guard lest

the vindictive herders set fire to the camps
or kill the sheep. These were no gentle children from the land of Mañana; we discovered
they were desperate characters from Old
Mexico, to whom murder was second nature.

Bill's opinion of the sheep business after
his brief experience in the camps could only
be published in an expurgated edition. He
hated the Mexicans, he hated the sheep, he
hated everything connected with them. After
seeing his charges safely on board a south-
bound train, he returned to the ranch with
all the joy of an exile.

"I've been up against tough men, Mrs.
Brook, but that bunch is the worst I ever
seen. They're just like a pack of coyotes,
grinnin' and sneakin' up behind you, waitin'
'til they git a chance to finish you. Between
listnin' to the grass grow and pickin' off
sheep ticks, I got plumb locoed settin' there
watchin' 'em. I jest had to feel my skin
every once in a while to be sure I wasn't
growin' wool."

IX

THE UNEXPECTED

IF there is anything in suggestion, Carlyle was responsible for the whole affair, otherwise *why* should we have deferred our drive until the late afternoon and selected *Sartor Resartus* of all books to read aloud after lunch?

Owen wanted to visit one of the sheep camps to examine the corrals before having the hay stacked there for winter use and he urged us to go with him. His invitation was joyfully accepted. For many weeks we had scarcely left the ranch as Owen's Mother, who was with us, had been desperately ill. The crisis had passed, however, so we did not hesitate to go off for a few hours, leaving Madame Brook with her nurse. My aunt, Owen's sister and her two children were at the ranch also, and after so many weeks of anxiety we all felt the relaxation and joy-

134

ously climbed into the wagon when Owen drove up.

There were summer and winter camps for the sheep and our objective point was an old place, acquired with the ranch, which had been converted into a winter camp. During the summer it was unoccupied.

We drove along laughing and talking. Owen's nephew carried his gun and kept a sharp lookout for coyotes. It was a glorious day and we were in the mood to appreciate all its beauty.

The meadows, waist deep in native hay, were flecked with the gold of the prairie sun flowers. The wild roses grew in tangled masses everywhere, their perfume mingled with the odor of the sage which yielded up its aromatic sweetness as the wheels crushed the silvery leaves. The plains were mottled with the shade of fleecy clouds which floated lazily across the sky, the changing lights flooded the hills with dazzling sunshine, then veiled them softly with faint cloud shadows. A delicate haze hung over the more distant hills, and behind the mountains thunderheads were gathering.

The road ran directly past the camp and long before we reached it we could see the old house, forbidding in its isolation, standing on a high mesa above the creek. It had been built years before by a settler named La Monte, whose footsteps misfortune had dogged until she overtook him at last. His wife deserted him and, broken in heart and fortune, he had left the country. Bohm held a mortgage on the place and it had passed into his possession.

An air of abandonment surrounded the camp even in winter when it was occupied, but during the summer when it was totally deserted the ghosts of dead happiness stalked unheeded through the silent rooms. Rank weeds filled the yards, the plaintive notes of the wood-doves in the cotton-woods by the creek and the weird, haunting howl of the coyotes were the only sounds to break the silence.

There was a tale connecting old Bohm with the La Monte tragedy for which an affair with Mrs. La Monte was responsible. We were some distance from the house, the rest of the party were intent on watching a big jack-rabbit which was bounding lightly across the prairie, but I was thinking of the wretched story which the sight of the old house always recalled, when the door was slowly opened and a naked man paused for a moment on the threshhold then walked down the steps into the yard.

I gave a gasp, my eyes fixed on that advancing figure, the others looked around but in that instant the man had seen us and dropped down into the tall weeds, by which he was completely hidden.

"What's the matter?" Owen asked, surprised by my exclamation.

"Why, Owen, a man without any clothes on just came out of that door and is there in the weeds."

Owen turned toward the yard, there was no one in sight; he looked at me in amazement. He knew I must be in earnest! I was not given to "seeing things".

"Why, that's absurd, how could you imagine anyone being out here in this deserted place miles and miles from the railroad?"

We were just opposite the house and as if in response to Owen's question the head and naked breast of a man rose up from behind the weeds. His face was crimson and the thick, black disheveled hair gave him such an aspect of wildness we were appalled.

Owen stopped the horses, the man rose to his feet, calmly looked at us, then turned and walked slowly into the house.

We were speechless. It was like a sudden apparition.

After a moment Owen passed the lines to me.

"Here, Esther, hold the horses while I go in and investigate."

"Be careful," was all I could say. There was a chorus of "Don'ts" from the back seat as he got out of the wagon.

I thought of the gun. "Gordon, take your gun and go after your uncle. I know that man is crazy."

Gordon jumped out and ran toward the house, but before he reached the door we heard a loud burst of singing, a curious rendering of "Ta-rah-rah boom-de-ahy". In a moment Owen and Gordon reappeared.

"Well, there's no doubt of his being crazy," Owen said, "we'll go to the Bosman ranch where I can get someone to come back with me. I can telephone the Sheriff from there, too." Then he told us what had happened.

By the time he reached the door the man had put on his outside shirt and was standing in the middle of the bedroom floor. He glared at Owen when he entered and made no reply when asked what he was doing there, then he turned around and walked over to an empty bed frame which stood against the wall, got behind it and gradually slipped down underneath. When he was lying flat on his back on the floor, his feet toward Owen, he began to sing in some broken foreign tongue.

It was uncanny and as we drove on toward the creek I could only say "What next?"

"I don't know what on earth can come next," Owen replied. "This is positively the most unexpected and unlikely thing that ever happened."

We had to drive down a hill before we crossed the creek and at last lost sight of the house, the sound of the wild singing grew more faint and finally died away.

There were no bridges in the country and while at this time there was no flowing water, the sand was wet. We drove down a steep bank into the bed of the creek and were almost across when without the slightest warning the bottom seemed to drop out of the earth beneath us and the wagon sank down.

"Quicksand!"

There was just time for that one exclamation in concert. Owen gave the horses a quick cut with the whip, they sprang forward, caught a footing on the solid sand and were safe. He gave them another cut, but pull as they would they could not move the wagon, which had sunk to the hubs. The double tree broke and the horses were free. Owen and Gordon jumped out on the tongue, holding onto the horses and drove them up the bank. There the rest of us sat, feeling the wagon sinking slowly farther and farther into the deadly, yielding substance.

The end of the wagon-pole rested on the firm sand, so by climbing over the dashboard holding on to it with one hand I was able to work my own way down the wagon tongue until I could grasp an outstretched hand and jump to safety. The others followed my example. The danger was past, but we trembled as we looked back.

It is impossible to distinguish quicksand from ordinary sand by its appearance, but it will not support the slightest weight. It seems to melt into nothing and the sensation is all the more terrifying from its suddenness. The first effect is instantaneous, then the engulfment becomes more gradual.

We were safe but afoot. Owen took the horses.

"Gordon and I will go on to the Bosmans and get another wagon. We won't be long and you women had better stay here and not walk these three miles."

I was just about to say "all right" when I happened to glance behind me and there on the bank, silhouetted quite sharply against the sky, stood the figure of a half-clad man.

He was watching every move we made.   I pointed to him.

"I think you'd better come with us," said Owen after one glance, "he might decide to investigate," and off we all trudged down the dusty road.

Blue black masses of cloud were spreading gradually across the sky and distant thunder muttered ominously.

If a bomb had alighted in the centre of the Bosman ranch, where supper was in progress, it couldn't have produced a more startling effect than our arrival on foot and the account of our experience.   They urged us to spend the night, as the storm was rapidly approaching, but we felt we must go back with Owen.

Mr. Bosman hitched our team to one of his wagons, while Owen telephoned to the Sheriff.   We took a few pieces of bread and meat for the poor demented creature at the camp and made another start.   Mr. Bosman and his son accompanied us on horseback.

We went by a different road to avoid crossing the creek.

It was dark by the time we reached the La Monte place, everything was still. The four men, with a lighted lantern, entered the house. A wild outburst of singing followed, which told us the same scene was being enacted. The men came out almost immediately, talking earnestly.

Mr. Bosman, an old-timer, had recognized the man as Jean La Monte, he had spoken to him, had called him by name, but no sign of understanding, not one faint glimmer of intelligence had shone from out those wild eyes. Mr. Bosman was almost overcome.

"It's just terrible to see him that way, he was such a good man. Poor old La Monte, trouble has sure driven him crazy. How on earth he ever got here beats me. There ain't a thing we can do tonight. We couldn't handle him if he got violent. There never was a stronger man in this country than Jean La Monte. My God! It's awful!"

So it was arranged that the Bosmans should go back to their ranch and send word to the Sheriff to be up there early in the morning and that Owen should have some of our men guard the place during the night.

"Poor devil, I don't believe he'll go away. He seemed so suspicious he wouldn't touch the bread, and I believe he's been here two or three days. See you in the morning," and the Bosmans disappeared in the darkness.

The thought of the tragedy with which we had so suddenly come in touch, weighed upon us. A living ghost connected us with a past in which we had no part.

Long after we had left the old place behind, the mad singing followed us, except when it was drowned by a sudden crash of thunder. The jagged flashes of lightning illuminated the heavens for a brief second, then left the world shrouded in an impenetrable darkness. Rather than risk going through the creek a second time, we had decided to cut across country.

The prairies were broken by deep gullies washed and torn by the fury of the summer storms. By day, driving was difficult; by night, it was hazardous in the extreme, and after a blinding flash which fairly tore the heavens apart, we were forced to stop the horses for fear of driving into an unseen gulch. The horses, headed toward home and excited and nervous, were hard to control. We drove along in silence, our staring eyes trying to pierce the darkness. It was so dangerous that at last I got out and walked in front of the horses. I could not see; I could only know from the contour of the ground when we were near a gulch or by my outstretched hand tell when we were near the wires of a fence. After a time Gordon took my place, and all the way one or the other walked before the team. The lightning and thunder were terrific, but still it did not rain. We were worn out with fatigue and anxiety when we finally reached the ranch.

Steve was standing with his saddle horse at the crossing of the creek, swinging a lighted lantern. When he heard the sound of the wheels he gave a shout.

"Mr. Brook!"

"All right," Owen called back. Steve came towards us.

"What on earth happened? We've all been plumb worried to death, and Madame Brook, she's most crazy. I've just sent Fred up to the La Monte place to look for you."

"La Monte place!" we exclaimed as several of the boys, attracted by Steve's shout, came up. "Get on your horse," said Owen, quickly, "and overtake him; there's a madman up there."

Steve did not wait for further instructions, but flung himself on his horse and tore off after Fred. We hurried in to reassure Owen's mother, who was nearly frantic. Later, as she bade us "Good-night," she said very seriously: "Owen, as soon as I am able I am going to Denver. I must be where it is quiet. I simply cannot stand the excitement here."

As the rain began to fall in torrents, we heard the men who had been detailed to guard the La Monte place galloping off.

An itinerant tailor had pulled into the ranch just before our return, and was peacefully sleeping in his wagon. He was awakened when the horses were driven into the corral, and came out to learn the cause of the commotion. He was so excited when he heard that an insane person was in the vicinity he asked to sleep at the bunk house with the men. They tried to laugh him out of his fears, but his fright was so genuine they told him to "come on."

The strangeness of the whole affair, the combination of circumstances and pure nervous and physical exhaustion kept Owen and me awake a long time. It seemed I had scarcely fallen asleep when I heard someone knock on the door and say:

"Mr. Brook, Mr. Brook."

I recognized Mary's voice, and responded for Owen, who was dead asleep.

"Mrs. Brook, the crazy man is down here at the corral; will you ask Mr. Brook to come out?"

It didn't take Owen long to dress. It was about five o'clock, and from the window we could see poor old La Monte, still attired in his shirt, sitting in the door of the granary playing with a little cotton-wood switch.

How he had escaped the men who had surrounded the place, and how he had found his way to our ranch were questions no one could answer.

The first intimation of his presence came in the form of a wild yell from the tailor, who had gotten up early and gone down to the corral to feed his horses. This brought all the men to the bunk house door as the terror-stricken little Jew flung himself into their arms.

"Mein Gott! Dot crazy man iss here."

"You're the only crazy man on this ranch," said Bill, taking him by the collar and giving him a shake. "What ails you, anyhow?"

"Oh, he iss here, he iss here," wailed the tailor. "He ain't got on no clothes, and we'll all be kilt." The boys left him and went out to investigate.

It was true. La Monte was there, and after a futile effort on Bill's part to get him to talk the boys retired to the bunk house and sent for Owen.

"Gee," Bill said later, "that feller was the doggondest lookin' thing I ever seen, settin' there in what was left of his shirt. His legs was all tore by the fence wires or brambles, his teeth was chatterin' and he was just blue with cold. His eyes had a look in 'em that give me the shivers. I don't wonder he scart that there Jew into a fit. I wasn't very anxious to come clost to him, neither. I ain't scart of anything that's human, but he ain't human, goin' 'round folks dressed like that." Bill was a stickler for convention.

"That's the first thing a person usually does when he goes crazy, Bill—takes off all his clothes."

Bill gave me an incredulous look.

"Gosh, I hope I'll be killed ridin' or somethin' and not lose my mind first. It ain't decent."

The poor demented creature would not speak nor pay any attention to the other men, but when he saw Steve he smiled as he asked:

"You've come to take me away from them, haven't you?"

"Yes," Steve said. "Will you go with me now?"

La Monte stood up.

"Yes, if you won't let them get me; those witches want to drag me back to hell, but I've fooled them this time. I've almost caught up with him once or twice and they drag me back." And he walked off quietly by Steve's side.

Steve took him to the bunkhouse, gave him some coffee and made him lie down on his bed. While Steve sat beside him La Monte slept fitfully, but at the slightest move started and tried to get up. Steve fell in with all his vagaries; he promised to help him escape the witches and to help him find the person for whom he seemed to be searching.

"Where was he last?" Steve asked, hoping to find some clue.

"Why, on his horse." La Monte sat up and stared wildly into Steve's eyes. "Don't you know, he's always on a horse, a big black horse. He's there just ahead of me, he's always just ahead of me," and he jumped up and started toward the door.

Steve calmed him again and he fell back on the pillows and lay there in silence, his eyes fixed on the ceiling.

Six crestfallen cow-punchers returned from the La Monte place. No one knew when the man had left the camp, no one had even caught a glimpse of him. His clothes they had found in the well.

The Sheriff and his posse came at last. Steve kept his hand on the arm of La Monte as they approached the wagon. It was a tense moment; we were all watching but hidden, fearful lest some trifle would arouse the demon of violence. The men were all armed.

La Monte put his foot up on the step of the wagon, then took it off, shook his head, turned and walked toward the granary. We held our breath. Steve alone followed him.

"Come on; you're going with me, aren't you?"

There was no reply. With his eyes fixed on the ground La Monte ignored Steve completely. Suddenly he stopped and picked up something, the little cotton-wood switch to which the leaves still clung. Holding it tightly, he walked back to the wagon, got in, Steve by his side, and they drove off.

They were scarcely out of sight when Charley came dashing up with sixty dollars in gold which he had found under a pile of mud at the La Monte place. Owen sent him to overtake the wagon.

"Is this yours?" Charley asked, as he rode up to them, holding the money out toward La Monte, who only shook his head and looked off across the prairie. Charley turned the money over to Steve.

When they reached the town, La Monte seemed to become confused and suspicious. He would not speak. He was judged insane and committed to the asylum. Still in charge of the Sheriff, Steve and two other men, he was put on the train.

"Where did you get him?" the conductor asked the Sheriff.

"Up in the country, at the A L ranch."

"Oh, yes, I know that place; it used to be the old Bohm——"

He never finished his sentence, for La Monte, with a cry, sprang to his feet, looked wildly about, brushed them aside and jumped through the window.

The train was stopped, and they ran back to where he had fallen. He had broken his leg, but in spite of that fought them off with superhuman strength. With the help of the train crew, he was overpowered at last, bound and taken back to the train.

Steve told us later it was the most terrible experience he had ever been through.

"I just couldn't stand the look in his eyes when they got him to the asylum. He didn't say nothin', just kept moanin' all the time. He'd been there for five years, and no one knew how he got away. I suppose it would a come anyhow, but it seemed like it was the mention of Bohm's name that set him off."

X

AROUND THE CHRISTMAS FIRE

WITHIN a radius of many miles there were only three small children, and about them our Christmas festivities revolved. They furnished the excuse for the tree, but no work was too pressing, no snow too deep to prevent the boys from bringing the Christmas tree and greens from a small clump of pines which stood on top of a distant hill, like a dark green island in the midst of the prairie sea.

Early on Christmas morning Steve started out with gaily bedecked baskets for the Mexicans, and at the ranch the greatest excitement prevailed. I dashed franctically between the bunkhouse and our kitchen to be certain that nothing was forgotten. The big turkeys were stuffed to the point of bursting, all the "trimmings" were in readiness, and the last savory mince pies were in the ovens.

© By Permission R. R. Doubleday

BUCKING HORSE AND RIDER

Behind the closed doors of the living room the tall tree, festooned with ropes of popcorn and garlands of gaudy paper chains, glittered and glowed with its tinsel ornaments and candles.

Owen divided his attention between his "Santa Claus" costume and pails of water, which he placed near the tree in case it should catch fire.

The boys spent most of the morning "slicking up" and put on their red neckties, the outward and visible sign of some important event, then passed the remaining hours sitting around anxiously awaiting the arrival of the guests of honor and—dinner.

Sometimes members of the family were with us or some friends were lured from the city by the promise of a "really, truly Christmas," and there were always a few lonely bachelors to whom the holidays, otherwise, would have brought only memories.

Christmas was our one great annual celebration, a day of cheer and happiness, in which everyone joyously shared. It was a new experience in the life of the undomesticated cow-puncher, but he took as much satisfaction in the fact that "Our tree was a whole lot prettier than the one I've saw in town" as though he had won a roping contest.

Each year the children and their parents were invited for Christmas dinner. They might be delayed en route by deep snow-drifts, out of which they had to dig themselves, but they always arrived eventually. We came to have a sincere affection for those children, gentle little wild flowers of the prairie.

They were very sweet, perfectly ingenuous, gazing in round-eyed wonder upon things which to most of us were commonplace.

I never thought of its being anything new in their brief experience until at dinner one of the small boys turned to his mother after tasting a piece of celery and said, "Look, Mamma, 'tain't cabbage and 'tain't onions. What is it?"

They positively trembled with excitement as they learned to read and laboriously spelled out the words in the simple books we gave them. They craved knowledge as a starving man craves bread.

As Santa Claus, Owen wore a ruddy mask with a long white beard and bristling eyebrows, a fur cap pulled down over his ears, heavy felt boots and his long fur overcoat. He looked and acted the part so perfectly the children for years insisted that "there is a Santa Claus 'cause we've seen him."

The first Christmas everyone was gathered about the tree waiting for this mysterious personage to appear when Owen suddenly thought of bells; he must have sleighbells. No self-respecting Santa Claus was complete without them. I was in despair; there wasn't a sleigh-bell within a hundred miles, but Owen insisted that he must jingle. At last after a great deal of argument and searching for something which would give forth bell-like sounds, he finally pranced out before the spell-bound audience with my silver table bell sewed to the top of one of his boots. He had to prance because the bell refused to tinkle unless it was shaken, and for the ensuing hour he pranced so vigorously that between the exercise and the fur coat he nearly perished from heat.

After dinner we all assembled in the big living-room, where my disguised husband presented each person with some little gift and ridiculous toy, accompanied by a still more ridiculous rhyme, over which the boys roared. They enjoyed the jokes most of all. No one escaped; Owen and I came in for our share with the rest. Mine usually bore veiled or open allusion to my particular pet lamb which had developed strong butting proclivities. He butted friend and foe indiscriminately, so that even my fond eyes were not blinded to his faults, and Owen's remarks were most uncomplimentary after he had acted as a shield for us when "Jackie" had chased my sister and me all about the yard.

Later in the afternoon everybody scattered—our house guests amused themselves as they chose, riding, driving or hunting coyotes, the boys rode over to the neighboring ranches or went to "town," the store and saloon at the railroad station sixteen miles away, but I spent an hour or two playing with the children or reading to them until their father "brought the team around," their happy mother climbed up on the high seat of the lumber-wagon and, clinging to dolls, trains and toys, three blissfully happy but perfectly exhausted little children were wrapped up in quilts and coats, stowed into the back of the wagon and started on the twenty-mile drive "back home."

It had been an eventful day in their short, barren lives, but for us it was the best part of Christmas, except the evening, when we all gathered about the big fireplace which drew everyone into its circle like a magnet.

There was nothing prosaic about those who grouped themselves around the great stone fireplaces on the ranches in the old days. Here again were found those contrasts, so striking and unexpected; university men who had come West for adventure or investment, men of wealth whose predisposition to weak lungs had sent them in exile to the wilderness, modest young

Englishmen, those younger sons so often found in the most out-of-the-way corners of the earth, and who, through the sudden demise of a near relative, had such a startling way of becoming earls and lords over night; adventurous Scotchmen, brilliant young Irishmen, all smoking contentedly there in the firelight and discussing the "isms" and "ologies" and every other subject under heaven. But most interesting of all were their own reminiscences.

We were all sitting around the fire one Christmas night when the conversation turned on adventure, and everyone promised to tell the most thrilling experience he had ever had.

Two of the men were lying on the big bearskin before the fire. One, a mining engineer, told of having been captured by bandits and held for a ransom, in some remote corner of Mexico where he had gone to examine a very famous mine. The other, a surveyor for the Union Pacific Railroad, had been lost during a storm and, becoming snow-blind, crawled for five miles on his hands and knees, feeling the trail with naked, half frozen hands until he reached the creek down which he waded until he came to the camp.

In a big chair, the firelight playing over her slender figure, sat Janet Courtland, an Eastern woman, who as a mere girl had come West with her young husband and had gone up into Montana where he had bought a large cattle ranch.

"Come on, Mrs. Courtland, you're next," the Surveyor said as he finished his story.

"Well," Janet began, "Will and I have had so many experiences I scarcely know which was the most exciting, but I think our encounter with the Indians was the most thrilling from first to last.

"Will had to go into Miles City on business and I went with him for great unrest had been reported among the Indians and he didn't want to leave me on the ranch alone. We had been in town only a few days when we heard that they were on the war path and Will felt he must go back to the ranch. He wanted me to stay in town, but I wouldn't. If he was going back I was going with him, so we started in the buck-board on that long eighty-five mile drive. I'll never forget it. The day was fearfully hot and we were constantly looking out for Indians. We had gone about half-way, when we came over the top of a hill and saw a band of Indians just below us. They saw us before we could turn back, we had to go on, and as we came towards them they formed into two lines so that we had to drive between them. It was horrible." And Janet gave a shiver at the recollection. "I'll never forget as long as I live those frightful, painted faces. Not an Indian moved; we passed through the line and had gone a short distance beyond, when we heard the report of a gun. Will clapped his hand to his side and said: 'My God, I'm shot. Drive as fast as you can'—and he threw the lines to me.

"I lashed the horses and we fairly tore. Everything was still, there was only that one shot, the Indians made no attempt to follow us. We did not speak. Will was lying back in the buckboard, his hand pressed to his side. When we had gone out of sight of the

Indians I stopped the horses and asked Will where he was struck.

" 'In the side; I can feel the blood oozing through my fingers,' he said. He took his hand away and gave an exclamation as he looked at it. It was wet but not with blood. We could not find the sign of a wound. We got out to investigate and discovered—that just as we passed the Indians the cork flew out of a bottle of root beer we had in the back of the buckboard and struck him in the side. Poor old Willie, no wonder he thought he was shot," and Janet smiled at her husband, who laughed with the rest of us.

"Now, Owen," he said, "I know some of the things you've been through, so you can't beg off," and Owen began his story.

"In the spring of '81 I came West to visit my brother, Ed., on his ranch in Wyoming. I was a tenderfoot, never having been on the plains before—and yet—I had scarcely arrived when I announced that the one thing I wanted to do was to kill a buffalo. He told me that if my heart was set on it I should have the chance, but that it was dangerous sport even for experienced hunters, as a buffalo frequently turns and gores the horse before it can get out of the way.

"The very next day the dead body of a professional hunter was brought to the ranch. He had wounded a buffalo bull which had turned, caught with his horn the horse he was riding, thrown him to the ground and gored the hunter to death. The sight of his mangled body was shocking and made a terrible impression on my mind, but my purpose was not changed.

"My brother assigned Al. Turpin the responsibility of serving as my guide. He was one of the best riders on the ranch, cool-headed and a good shot. We took breakfast before daylight in order to get an early start. After riding a considerable distance three dark objects were discovered far away on a hill which sloped toward us. A pair of field glasses confirmed the opinion that they were buffalo lying down. We rode in their direction and kept out of sight, except as we peered cautiously over the top of each succeeding ridge until it was possible to approach no nearer in concealment, when we rode to the top of the nearest hill and were in full view. The buffalo saw us and quick as lightning were on their feet running away. We sent our horses at full speed down the slope, across a level piece of ground and up the hill after them. We were gaining rapidly. My horse was the faster of the two and was in the lead. He was one of the best trained cow ponies I have ever ridden and was my brother's favorite for cutting out cattle.

"When about thirty yards behind the buffalo, one stopped. The bit I was using was severe. I pulled and threw my horse back on his haunches. The buffalo was an immense bull. He appeared to me as big as a mountain. He turned facing me, his body at an angle, cocked his head on the side, then threw it toward the ground and, quicker than a flash, came down the hill like a landslide.

"My horse struggled against the bit and tried to jump toward the buffalo and turn him as he would a steer. I tried to swing his head away and dug my spurs into his sides to make him move, but he did not understand why he should run from a buffalo. He did respond a little and turned so that his haunches were toward the great brute coming down the hill.

"The head of the buffalo was in striking distance. He looked like a great devil. His beadlike eyes flashed fire. The next instant I expected the horse to be pitched down the hill. I could feel myself thrown into the air and then gored to death when I struck the ground. I could see the mangled body of the dead hunter.

"While my six-shooter was a powerful gun, I knew that if I should shoot the brute in the head, the ball would not go through the mass of matted hair and the thick skull. Still there was nothing else to do. I thought my time had come. In order to hit him at all it was necessary to shoot over my left arm. In my haste I pulled the trigger too soon. The loud report startled the horse into a run and turned the buffalo. Its discharge, so near my head, gave me a terrible shock. I thought the shot had blown away all the right side of my head and I put up my hand to keep my brains from falling out, but there were neither brains nor blood on my hand. The bullet had just grazed my head and gone through the rim of my hat. That brute looked like an infuriated demon. I couldn't have been more frightened if I had met the devil himself at the mouth of hell.

"When it was all over, I was not in a mood for challenging him again, but as he loped away, Al. ran his horse abreast and from a safe distance put a shot into his brisket. He fell dead. Believe me, I have had many close calls, but that was the one time in all my life when I was really scared."

"What extraordinary experiences people do have in this country," Will Mason exclaimed, as he leaned forward to light a fresh cigar. "Speaking of Ed. reminds me of a strange coincidence which happened the year after he came West.

"We had been together the year before in New York, where we had met a chap named Courtney Drake. He was a Yale man and a member of the University Club, so we saw quite a good deal of him. He was very congenial and one of the most lovable fellows I ever knew. He was married but he seldom spoke of his wife and we never met her.

"One morning we picked up the paper and were horrified to read that Mrs. Courtney Drake had shot her maid. There it was in glaring headlines, the whole wretched affair. The Drakes were one of the oldest and wealthiest families in New York and it was spicy reading for the scandal lovers I assure you.

"It seems that Drake had gotten mixed up with this woman when he first came out of college and in order to force him to marry her she told him that she was soon to have a child. He wouldn't believe it, and how she worked it I don't know. She must have been mighty clever, for she and her maid got hold of a baby somewhere and she made Courtney believe it was hers and that he was the father—so he married her.

"They had only been married a short time when the maid began to demand large sums of 'hush money' and Mrs. Drake gave her whatever she asked, for she was in mortal dread of having Drake discover the truth. The girl found blackmail so profitable she became more and more insistent in her demands and nearly drove Mrs. Drake wild. At last she could endure it no longer and in a perfect frenzy, shot and killed the maid and then the whole thing came out. Mrs. Drake was sent to prison, where she died later, but Courtney vanished utterly after the trial—no one knew what became of him.

"The next fall Ed. and I came West and two years later were up in the Jackson's Hole country with a party, shooting. Ed. and one of the guides went out one morning to get some ducks, but in a short time they came back to camp carrying the dead body of Courtney Drake. They had come across his body on the shore of a small lake, lying face down in the mud. There was a single bullet hole in the back of his head.

"Think of his having been found out there in the wilderness by the only man in the country who knew who he was! Talk about chance," Will sighed, "Poor devil, he was living out there under an assumed name.

His family had no idea where he was. Ed. notified them and then took his body East.

"Just after his death Drake's partner produced a bill of sale for the entire ranch and took possession of it. Everyone suspected him of the murder, but it couldn't be proved. About three years later the man killed his wife and at the time of his conviction the question of Drake's murder was brought up and he confessed. Isn't it strange the way things happen?" Will's question was general. "What on earth do you suppose sent Ed. Brook into the Jackson's Hole country at that one time of all others?"

No one answered.

"I wonder if all new countries abound in such tragic mysteries?" The Surveyor looked up at me.

"What tragic mysteries have you encountered, Mrs. Brook, that makes you speak so feelingly?"

Just then the clock struck twelve and I got up.

"It's too late for more mysteries, it's time to go to bed—and we don't want tragedies to keep us wide awake on Christmas night."

"Oh, come on Esther, tell us your most thrilling experience," they begged. "We won't move a step until you do."

"Marrying Owen," I replied, looking over at my unsuspecting husband, "I've never had a chance to get my breath since."

And amid a shout of laughter the Christmas party broke up.

XI

TED

TED landed in our midst with all the attendant violence of a meteor.

He didn't arrive, he landed, bag and baggage, and until his departure weeks later our tranquil existence was sufficiently hectic to suit even Bill.

After numerous letters from his doting aunt, we reluctantly consented to look after Ted while she was in Europe recuperating from a nervous break-down. At the end of the first week, we understood why Aunt Elizabeth found recuperation necessary, and I suggested to Owen, it might be well to engage our passage on a later steamer, for I had a premonition that my own nerves might require a rest after two months of Ted's strenuous companionship.

He wasn't bad; there was not a bad thing about him. He was just overflowing with

youth and energy, which had been pent up
for years, between boarding school in the
winter and Newport in the summer.

Motherless, fatherless, rich, neglected or
over-indulged by a none too wise aunt, Ted
was an appealing young person, a character
easily to be made or marred by circumstances.

He looked like a member of the celestial
choir—blue-eyed, fair-haired and mild—but
he produced the effect of a Kansas cyclone.

There was nothing he did not see, there
was nothing he did not hear and there was
nothing he did not do. Even on eighty thousand acres of land his activities were somewhat limited.

He was wildly enthusiastic about the West,
fascinated by the men, and was Bill's
shadow, so we promptly turned him over to
those "rough persons" Aunt Elizabeth had
especially hoped that he might avoid, to get
it all out of his system.

"Let him stay at the bunk-house," Owen
advised after Ted had besought me to allow
him to stay with the men. "It will do him

more good than anything else in the world, if he has the right stuff in him."

Ted stood on the porch, uneasily shifting from one foot to the other, when I came out of the office.

"All right, Ted, Mr. Brook and I are perfectly willing for you to stay with the men, if you really want to."

He hopped up and down and almost embraced me in his joy.

"Oh, thank you, Mrs. Brook." "You see," he explained, carefully, "I've seen people like you and Mr. Brook all my life, but I never had the chance to be with real cow-punchers before. Evidently, from Ted's point of view, Owen and I were very commonplace individuals compared to these heroes of the prairie, and I laughed to myself as he bounded down the steps to break the joyful news to Bill that he was to share his bed and board.

The next day we had to go to town to meet some prospective wool buyers, and, after having his breakfast interrupted five different times by Ted's dashing in to see if we were ready, Owen was moved to inquire finally, "What on earth is on the boy's mind now?"

"His outfit," I answered. "He's been planning it for days; wishes to select it himself and we are not to see it until we get home."

That was a wise stipulation of Ted's, for if we had seen it, we should never have been able to get home.

He put it on as soon as we reached the ranch, and when he finally emerged, the flaming sunset paled with chagrin at its futile effort of years.

The "outfit" consisted of tan corduroy trousers, chaps of long silky angora wool, which had been dyed a brilliant orange, a shirt of vivid green, a bright red silk handkerchief for his neck, an enormous Stetson hat, high-heeled tan boots, silver studded belt and huge spurs.

We gasped when we saw him, but he was so intent on showing himself to Bill, as to be utterly unconscious of the effect he produced.

We followed him into the yard where the boys were waiting the call to supper. Bill looked up from the quirt he was braiding and blinked.

"Gosh! I thought the sun had set an hour ago," he remarked.

"No," Ted laughingly responded, giving him a push, "but he's going to 'set' now," and he threw himself down by Bill's side. "I knew you fellows would guy me, but all the same I think this outfit's great," and he surveyed himself with infinite pride and satisfaction.

"It's all right," said Bill, taking in all the details of the resplendent costume, and looking up at Owen and me with twinkling eyes, "I like somethin' a little gay myself; but round here where everything's green, we won't be able to tell you from a bunch of soap-weed," and Ted good naturedly joined in the laugh at his own expense.

"Wouldn't his Aunt Elizabeth die of heart-failure if she could see him now?" I asked Owen as we went into the house.

"She certainly would," he answered, "but we'll trust to luck and let Nature take its course."

Everything, including Nature, took its course rapidly with Ted, and for the next few weeks wise prairie dogs, rabbits and rattle-snakes stayed in their holes. By the end of his stay that energetic young person had enough rattle-snake skins to provide belts and hat-bands for all of New York, and scores of live prairie-dogs he had trapped to be shipped to his aunt's place in Newport.

I tried to picture the joy of Aunt Elizabeth and her neighbors when they found informal prairie-dog towns in the midst of their formal gardens. If life is measured by experiences, a few additional years were in store for Newport.

Bill taught Ted to shoot and he spent hours and a fortune shooting at old tin cans on a post before Bill finally consented to say:

"I've saw fellers do worse," the sweetest praise that ever fell on mortal ears, judging by Ted's expression.

And, then, Owen went to New Mexico to buy some sheep and Bohm came to sleep on a claim.

This claim was one over which Owen and

Bohm had been having a controversy for months. It had been included in the sale of the ranch, and after one of our most important sheep camps had been built upon it, Owen discovered that Bohm could not give a deed to it, as he had not made final proof on the land.

Bohm never ceased to regret having sold the ranch, and had never forgiven Owen for buying it and making him live up to his contract, so was only too glad of the opportunity to cause him all the trouble possible. Time after time he promised to come out and "prove up", but he never came, so although I was most anxious to have him come, I was far from pleased to have him about when Owen was away.

Ted, however, was overjoyed; he seemed to feel that Providence had arranged Bohm's visit to the ranch for his especial entertainment, and from the moment the old chap arrived Ted dogged his footsteps.

At first, old Bohm seemed quite flattered and laughed and joked with him, praised his shooting, told him stories of the Indian days,

promised to show him the underground
passage to an abandoned stage station, but
later he became annoyed, for no clinging burr
ever clung more closely than Ted. He
scarcely allowed Bohm to get out of his sight
for one moment.

How much the boy had heard of old
Bohm's history I did not know, but I concluded a few rumors had reached those ever-
attentive ears, for one day he came in fairly
beaming.

"Gosh! Pudge and Soapy haven't got anything on me, they've only seen Buffalo Bill
in a show, and I'm right in the same house
with a man that's a holy terror!"

"What do you mean, Ted?" I asked,
anxious to find out how much he had heard.

"Oh, you know well enough, Mrs. Brook,"
he laughed, going to the door as he saw old
Bohm on his way to the barn. "You can't
fool me. Gee! I wouldn't have missed him
for the world. The fellows'll just be sick
when I tell them."

"The fellows" were evidently "Pudge" and
"Soapy", his two chums at St. Paul's,

"Pudge" because of "his shape," as Ted explained, and "Soapy", whose parental millions came from the manufacturing of soap.

The game between the boy and Bohm was amusing. Clever as the old chap was, he couldn't evade Ted's watchful eye. If Bohm thought him miles away, he suddenly appeared with such an unconscious air of innocence he disarmed all suspicion, but he made Bohm uneasy.

"Quit campin' on the old man's trail, Kid," said Bill one evening at the corral after Ted had driven Bohm to the bunk-house to escape his questions. "You're gettin' on his nerves; let him go and sleep on his claim and get through with it. You and me's got to hunt horses tomorrow, anyways."

Ted cheerfully acquiesced, and old Bohm loaded his wagon alone and drove toward his claim in peace.

The next morning very early, I heard Bill calling Ted. No Ted appeared, and I went out to see where he was.

"Where do you reckon that crazy kid's went now?" demanded Bill, impatient to start.

"I'm sure I don't know, Bill, hunting prairie-dogs, probably. Don't wait for him, if you're ready to go."

"Huntin' prairie-dogs," echoed Bill. "I'll bet a hat he's huntin' old Bohm somewheres." He frowned as he cinched up his saddle. "I reckon I'd better ride over that way and see what he's up to."

"I wish you would," I said, vaguely uneasy. "I don't want him to bother Bohm too much."

"Me neither," said Bill, getting on his horse, "there's his pony's tracks now," he looked at the ground. "I'll find him and take him along with me. Don't you worry, he's all right, but he sure is a corker—that kid," and Bill galloped off.

I felt confident that he would overtake the lad, so I dismissed them all from my mind and settled down to an uninterrupted morning, and a delayed postal report.

I was busy all day and was just starting out for a little walk before supper when Bill and Ted rode up.

Bill and Ted, hatless, clothes torn and

covered with dirt and blood, their faces scratched and bruised, and Ted regarding me triumphantly from one half-closed eye, the other being swollen shut.

"What on earth hap—" I tried to ask, my breath fairly taken away. Bill got off his horse and came up to the gate.

"We're all right, Mrs. Brook. I'm sorry you seen us 'fore we got fixed up a little; we just got mixed up some with Bohm—that's all—'taint nothin' serious. We look a whole lot worse than we feel, don't we Ted?"

"You bet we do," mumbled Ted from a cut and bleeding mouth, "but you ought to see Bohm, he's a sight!"

Ted got off his horse with difficulty. "Gosh, it was great," he said, leaning up against the fence for support.

"Come in and sit down, both of you, Charley will take your horses," and I led the way into the house followed a little unsteadily by Bill and Ted, who collapsed on the first chairs they could reach.

I gave them some wine, washed off their blood-stained faces, and made protesting Ted go into my room and lie down. He was very pale, and I saw that he was faint.

I came back into the kitchen.

"Now, Bill, tell me about it. What happened and where is Bohm?"

"On his way back to Denver in the baggage car," announced Bill, draining the last drop from the glass he still held in his hand.

I started, "Oh, Bill, you didn't kill him?"

"No, but I wisht I had," he said calmly. He'd oughter be dead, the old skunk, trying to poison all them sheep."

"Poison the sheep; what sheep?"

"Your sheep," Bill's brows contracted as he looked at me. "Your sheep," he repeated, his voice rising as I scarcely seemed able to grasp his meaning. "All the sheep at Hay Gulch Camp, that's what he came out here for, and he'd a done it, too, if it hadn't been for that kid in there." Bill jerked his head in the direction of my room.

"Ted?" I asked, my emotion stifling my voice.

"Ted," Bill affirmed, "he caught him at it red-handed, and probably saved two thousand sheep from bein' dead this minute."

"How on earth did he find it out?"

"Bill straightened up in his chair.

"Them eyes a his'n don't miss much, I'm here to tell you, and his everlastin' snoopin' around done some good after all." Bill's eyes glowed with pride. "Yesterday, before Bohm left, Ted come acrost him mixin' a lot of stuff with some grain, and, of course, had to know all about it. The old man finally told him he was fixin' to poison the prairie-dogs on his claim, but he was so peevish about it, Ted said he didn't believe him, and mistrusted somethin' was wrong."

"The kid didn't say nothin' to me about it; had some fool notion about playin' detective, I reckon, at any rate he got up along about four o'clock and rode out to Bohm's claim to do a little reconorterin'."

Bill reluctantly put the glass down and tipped back in his chair. "He hid his horse in the gulch and crope up in the grass like an Injin. The herder wasn't nowhere in sight and the sheep was still in the corral, but old Bohm was there all right, fixin' little piles of that poisoned wheat just where the sheep would come acrost it the first thing."

"Oh, Bill, that's the worst thing I ever heard!" I was sick at the mere thought.

Bill was too engrossed to pay any attention to the interruption.

"Ted said he was comin' back to tell me, but he got so excited when he seen what Bohm was up to, he never thought of nothin' but stoppin' him. The old man was stoopin' over with his back to Ted, and the kid gave a yell for the herder and ran for Bohm and before he could straighten up Ted was on top of him."

Bill scarcely paused for breath—"the old man reached for his gun, but Ted was too quick for him and knocked it out of his hand, and when I came up, there they was rollin' all over the prairie, first one on top and then the other."

Bill looked toward the door of my room, reflectively—"I kinder felt there was somethin' wrong when I left here, and believe me, I didn't spare my cayuse none gettin' there neither, and I didn't get there none too soon."

I was incapable of speech. I just stared at Bill.

"There ain't no doubt about Bohm's bein' ready to kill him; he was on top then and reachin' for his throat. I didn't stop to ask no questions. I jest grabbed him, and pulled him off of Ted. He was white as chalk and ready to eat us both alive, but I hung on to him while Ted got up cryin', 'Look what he's done, Bill, look what he's done,' and pointed at somethin' on the ground."

Bill's eyes were like two live coals. "Bohm was cussin' like a steam engine 'bout the kid's jumpin' him when he was puttin' out poison for the prairie-dogs. I just took one look around and seen all them piles of poison wheat there by the corral when there wasn't a prairie-dog within two miles. I—well, I aint goin' to tell you what I said, Mrs. Brook, 'taint fit for you to hear."

Bill looked down and turned the glass on the table around and around. He looked up again and smiled, but his brows contracted as he went on—"We had words then, sure enough. All of a sudden Bohm made a lunge and caught the handkerchief round my neck with one hand and reached for somethin' with the other, and the first thing I knew he was slashin' at me with a pocket knife. I guess I saw red then, 'cause I knocked him down and nearly pounded the life out of him."

Bill stopped a moment—"His eyes was rollin' back in his head and his tongue was hangin' out and there was a pool of blood 'round us, three yards across." Bill's description was so vivid I shut my eyes. "I reckon I'd killed him if Ted hadn't tromped my legs and kinda brought me to myself. He'd oughter been killed, but I let him up then and told Ted to go for my rope. We tied his hands and legs. I guess he had about all he wanted for he wasn't strugglin' much." Bill smiled grimly. "We carried him into the cabin, and there was the Mexican lying in his bunk—doped. We knew who done it all right, and I tell you we didn't handle Bohm like no suckin' infant when we laid him down, neither."

Bill's face was stern and set and I shared

his indignation too much to trust myself to speak.

"We left him there and went to get the wheat out of the way before we opened the corral gates for the sheep. Thanks to Ted, Bohm hadn't had time to put much around. He's a great little kid, that boy." Bill's voice broke.

"Bless his heart," I said, my own heart filled with gratitude and tenderness for the plucky little chap in the other room. Bill's eyes were moist, but his voice was steady again.

"Steve and Charley came up just then with the supply wagon, so Steve set Charley to herd the sheep. We loaded Bohm into the wagon and Steve took him over to the railroad. He said he'd see he got on the train all right." Bill grinned, "You're rid of Bohm for good now, Mrs. Brook, for I kinda think he gathered from what me and Steve said the ranch wouldn't be no health resort for him if he ever showed his ugly face round here again."

"Oh, Bill, I'm so thankful; it makes me

© *Rocky Mountain Photo Co.*

FACING DEATH EACH TIME THEY RIDE A NEW HORSE

sick when I think what might have happened."

"Don't thank me, Mrs. Brook, I ain't done nothin'." Bill's face was red with embarrassment as he stood up. "Ted's the one to thank, he's some kid, believe me," and Bill's eyes were very tender.

"Let's go in and see how he's making it." Bill followed me into the room.

Ted was sitting up on the couch, regarding his battered visage in my hand-glass with the greatest interest. I could see at once he was in no mood for emotion or petting.

"Hello, I'm all right," he murmured with a one-sided grin. "Say, Bill, wasn't it great? I wouldn't have missed it for a million dollars." He sank back with a sigh of supreme satisfaction. "I just wish I could remember all the things he called me. I want to spring them on the fellows when I go back."

Bill looked at him with genuine concern. "See here, kid," he said decidedly, "you want to forget all them things as quick as you can. Don't you go springin' any such language back where you come from. I'm no innocent

babe myself, but I'm here to tell you old
Bohm's cussin' made anything I ever heard
sound like a Sunday School piece. You forget it now, pronto," he commanded as he
went out of the door. "It's a reflection on
me and Mrs. Brook."

After Bill had gone, Ted looked at himself
again, then at me. "What do you suppose
Aunt Elizabeth would say if she could see me
now?" We both laughed.

"I would be a 'disgrace to my family and
position' now, sure enough." He felt his
blackened eye tenderly.

I sat down on the couch beside him. "You
will never be more of a credit to your family
than you are at this minute, Ted, nor more of
a man."

He looked up, for my voice shook a little.
He knew what I meant and his lips twitched
as he patted my hand gently, and turned his
face away.

XII

BLIZZARDS

IT was just like Louise Reynolds to arrive on the wings of a blizzard, wearing a straw hat and spring suit. Louise led the seasons, she never followed them, and she preceded that particular storm by about two hours; but she was justified, for it was April and she was on her way from California.

In this land of the unexpected even the weather disregarded all established precedents. A glorious Indian Summer night extended into January, or a sudden blizzard would swoop down from the North in October or April and leave us snowed in for days.

That is exactly what happened upon this occasion and most of Louise's visit was spent in shovelling snow for the pure joy of the exercise. That energetic young person had to do something in lieu of tennis or golf.

The prairies were covered with a fluffy mantle of purest white, great drifts filled the gulches and the roads were utterly obliterated. Long after the storm the men had to go about on horseback for no wagon could be moved through the deep snow.

At this juncture Louise announced that she had all of her reservations through to Baltimore, where she was to officiate as bridesmaid. She was obliged to go and we had to take her to the railroad.

We could scarcely go on horseback with baggage, there wasn't a sleigh in the country, certainly none on the ranch, but if Necessity was the Mother of Invention, Owen was a near relative. He never failed to find some way of meeting the most difficult problem. If Louise must go it devolved upon him to see that she reached the station and so he produced a sled, a disreputable old affair, used for the exalted purpose of hauling dead animals to "the dump"—but still it was a sled and under Owen's direction it was scrubbed and transformed into the most luxurious equippage by having a packing box nailed on the back and covered with rugs. Louise and I perched on the box, with heavy robes tucked in about us, the suit cases were at our feet and Owen sat on the trunk in front to drive.

There was only one draw-back, the sled had no tongue to keep it from running on to the heels of the horses, so Owen cut a hole in the bottom of the sled through which he stuck a broom-stick. My task was to work this improvised brake when we went down hill by jabbing the broom-stick into the snow. It worked beautifully except that the friction against the hard snow broke pieces of it off and it grew perceptibly shorter as we advanced.

In order to avoid some especially deep gulches we left the valley and followed a high ridge. It was much longer, but we had allowed the entire day for the trip. There was no danger of becoming lost as long as we could see, for we knew too well the country and the general direction to be followed.

No incident marred the joy of that day. When the horses floundered and almost disappeared from sight in a snow-filled gulch, leaving the sled stranded like an Ark on a gleaming Ararat, we had only to dig the horses out with a shovel which had been taken for the purpose and after getting them on the level ground, go back and hitch a long rope to the sled, draw it across the gulch and proceed upon our way.

The light of the sun upon the snow was so intense it was necessary to wear colored glasses to avoid snow blindness, and being muffled in furs, we looked like three bears in goggles. Our wraps kept us perfectly warm and it was a merry ride. The adventure filled us with joy as we glided over the trackless world in which we alone moved.

There was no suggestion of dreariness or desolation in the scene. Under the magic touch of the sun the world burst forth into a miracle of glory and beauty which held us spellbound. The sky was cloudless, not a shadow fell across that dazzling white expanse, which flashed and sparkled with all the prismatic colors. Far to the west Pike's Peak stood, a marvel of varying lights and shadows, its head resting on the soft blue bosom of the sky. Its commanding height had filled the Indian of the Plains with worshipful awe, it was to him "the Gate of Heaven, the abiding place of the Great Spirit." According to his own testimony, the one inevitable duty in the life of the Indian is the duty of prayer—and how often as he looked upon that distant mountain must the red hunter have paused in the midst of the vast prairies, his soul uplifted and an unspoken prayer on his lips!

The whole aspect of the country was changed, all the familiar landmarks were gone. Except for the hills, the surface of the prairie was perfectly level as though the Great Spirit had stretched his hand forth from that mystic mountain and passing it over the world had left it smooth and stainless.

It was a wonderful experience, and when toward evening we reached the railroad we were thrilled and triumphant over our accomplishment. The night was spent in the little four-room "hotel," we saw Louise safely on board the eastbound express the next morning, then returned to the ranch.

To be out after a blizzard is one thing, to be out in one is quite another, and we always grew apprehensive when the sky became suddenly overcast and the snow began to fall from leaden clouds. What if the storm should catch the herders and the sheep too far away from the camp?

They were all warned to range their sheep to the North if it threatened to storm, as most of the blizzards came from that direction and the sheep would go before the wind back to camp and safety. But they will not face it and, if unmindful of his orders, the herder took them South and a sudden storm came, he could not turn his sheep back to the camp; they would drift on and on before the wind, sometimes plunging over a bank to be buried beneath the drifting snow or piling up and smothering each other.

One winter just as Owen and I were starting home from California we received a telegram from Steve saying that during a bliz-

zard the buck herd had been lost. Owen had
some very important business which detained
him when we reached Denver, so he asked
me to go on to the ranch, have Steve organize
the men into searching parties and look
through every gulch in the vicinity for any
discolored holes on the top of the drifts which
would be caused by the breath of the sheep
if they were under the snow. For two days
the men searched and finally came to a deep
bank of snow on the top of which were found
the discolored holes they sought; they dug
down and discovered the bucks. A few had
been smothered, but most of them were
taken out alive after having been buried for
ten days! During the storm the herder had
left them and the poor distracted things had
drifted over an embankment and were en-
tombed under the snow.

When anyone speaks of "good-for-nothing
Mexicans" I think of Fidel, a mere lad, who
had taken his sheep South on a clear morning, but was overtaken by a storm before he
could get them back to the corrals. He and
his dog did everything they could do to turn

them, but they drifted farther and farther away. Fidel stayed with them, guiding them away from the gulches until they reached a railway cut. There Steve found them twenty-four hours later when we feared that Fidel had perished with his sheep. Facing death alone in the freezing wind and blinding, smothering snow, hour after hour he had kept his sheep from piling up. He not only saved them all, but they were in better condition than many in the corrals at the camps. Not for a moment had he left them. His hands and feet were frozen; he barely escaped freezing to death and on that day we learned the true meaning of "Fidelity."

Then once more Fate took a hand in our affairs and a blizzard changed the whole course of our lives.

We owned our land and no one could encroach upon us, but after a few years we began to notice forlorn little shacks built here and there on the open range by the poor home-seekers who, attracted by the prospect of free land, had begun "homesteading."

They built flimsy little houses, scratched up the surface of the prairie for a few inches and raised pitiful, straggling crops. The settlers were coming in! The opening wedge of that great onrush had been thrust deep into the heart of the prairie. In the undisputed possession of our own land we were not disturbed. While we knew that it meant the occupation of the free range and the passing of the large ranches, eventually, we scarcely realized how soon it would come and were not prepared to receive an offer from an Eastern syndicate to buy the entire ranch —to cut it into small units to be sold as farms.

The era of "dry-farming" had just begun, when by scientific methods, deep ploughing and the conservation of all moisture, dry land might be successfully cultivated without irrigation. It was a dream of the future of the prairie region, impossible to visualize, and I laughed in my ignorance, as Owen read me the letter.

"How perfectly absurd. Imagine trying to farm out here; the grangers would starve to death in a year unless they had stock of some sort. Surely you would never think of selling out?"

"I don't know, Esther, the homesteaders can't come on to our deeded land, but they are filing on all the Government land. In a short time there will be no more free range, and did you ever stop to consider that our land will soon be so valuable that we can't afford to run sheep on it?"

In that last sentence I saw the handwriting on the wall. It was only a question of time and this phase, too, of our life would pass.

In the East life seems to be static, but in the West it is in a state of flux and conditions are constantly changing.

Perhaps I had inherited the static state of mind for I had taken it for granted that all the rest of our days were to be spent there on the ranch under the shadow of the mountain. Suddenly a realization of the facts swept over me. In a sense we had been pioneers, we had blazed a trail that others were to follow and like the Indians we, too, were destined to move on. However, before you are thirty to regard yourself as a hoary-headed pioneer requires a series of mental gymnastics and, while my brain was going through a few preparatory exercises, I did not take the question of selling out very seriously. After all those years of struggle just as it had been brought to perfection, after we had put into it the best of our life, youth, energy and work, a part of our very selves, it did not seem possible that we could part with the ranch. Owen felt much as I did, but he was the first to realize that we had come again to the parting of the ways and that a decision must be made.

Yet—in the end—it wasn't the financial consideration nor a deep conviction that the future development of the country would be retarded if we remained, but an unexpected blizzard which turned the scale and set us adrift again.

The sun rose clear on the 19th of October, but during the morning it began to grow cloudy.

Owen and several of the men were at the railroad station where they were shipping lambs. During the afternoon the wind began to blow, it grew much colder and snow fell.

The next morning it was storming very hard and Steve, after arranging to have hay hauled to the various camps, went out on horseback to see that all the sheep were kept in the corrals. I was greatly relieved when Owen got home in the middle of the afternoon. Ten thousand lambs had been loaded and started on their way in spite of the storm, but the drive back to the ranch had been very hard, for hour by hour the storm increased in fury. The ground was covered and even the dull grey sky was hidden by dense clouds of powdery snow which did not seem to fall upon the earth but was blown in long horizontal lines across the prairies by the force of a mighty gale. It filled the gulches and piled in deep drifts. It was driven against the house with such force it sifted through the smallest crack. The windows on the North and West were covered with a solid coating of snow, the wind whistled and moaned and tore at the shutters as if trying to carry them with it on a wild race over the plains. It was impossible to see the corrals, even the garden fence was lost behind the driving, swirling snow. To open the door was to inhale a freezing gust of snow-laden air, millions of icy particles blinded the eyes and took away the breath.

We knew that the sheep were all in the corrals, but we feared that unless the herders watched them carefully they would pile up as the snow drifted over the high sides of the inclosure. The rest of the stock was protected and my heart was filled with thankfulness that Owen and the men had been able to reach the ranch. They went about the place like white wraiths doing the necessary things. Above the howling of the wind not a sound could be heard; a shout was carried miles away as soon as it left the lips. By five o'clock it was dark.

About eight o'clock, Mary came in and told Owen that Steve wanted to see him. When Owen returned, instead of coming into the living-room, he went to the closet, took down

his short, fleece-lined riding coat and began
to put it on.

"What's the matter, Owen, you are not
going out?"

"I must," he said, quietly, winding a long
scarf about his neck, "Steve says that Dorn
went out yesterday afternoon with a load of
hay for the camp on Six Shooter; he should
have come back last night or certainly this
morning. He's new and doesn't know the
country and he may be lost. I'm going to
see if I can find him."

My heart stood still; the camp on Six
Shooter gulch was fully eight miles away.
Eight miles in that storm! It did not seem
possible that a man could live to go a mile.

"Oh, Owen, I can't let you go! Don't you
suppose he is at the camp?"

"I don't know, he may be, but I must go
and find out. We can't take a chance on a
man's being lost." In the face of that argument there was nothing to say and nothing
to do but accept it.

"Who is going with you?"

"No one"—Owen did not look at me as he

answered—"I can't ask any of the men to face this storm."

I understood; he couldn't require any of his men to risk their lives. A hand of ice closed about my heart and deadened every sensibility. Like a machine I went about helping Owen get ready and at last went to the kitchen to bring him some coffee just before he left. A man was standing by the door muffled in wraps. I stood still.

"Why, Bill, where have you been?"

"I ain't 'been', I'm goin'. I'm goin' with Mr. Brook. A man ain't got no business out a night like this alone."

"Bill!" It was all I could say—but he understood.

When Owen came out he tried to dissaude him, but Bill was determined.

"I know I don't have to go, Mr. Brook, you never asked me, but I'm a goin', there ain't nothin' can keep me."

I had never seen him so serious, all the old half bantering tone was gone and they went out together, master and man, each risking his life for the sake of another.

I tried to watch them but instantly they were lost to my sight as a vague grey cloud closed about them.

How the night passed I do not know. I kept the fires up and the coffee hot and walked miles, back and forth, back and forth. I did not think of sleeping. It was useless to try to read. I could not see the words—the printed page was blank and I could only see the figures of two men on horseback, beaten, buffeted, fighting for their lives against the cruel snow-laden gale. I saw them separated, perhaps, trying to get through the gulches on their floundering horses, or walking to keep from freezing and then perhaps exhausted—lying down to rest while that last deadly sensation of sleepiness crept over them.

Daylight came at last, but still I walked. I pushed my breakfast away untasted and tried to occupy myself with the duties of the day. I felt as though I should scream aloud if that howling wind did not cease, but hour after hour passed and there was no other sound. The men came and went about their work quietly, speaking but little and then in subdued tones as in the presence of death; over us all hung the pall of terrifying uncertainty.

When occasionally it was possible to catch a glimpse of the corrals or the blacksmith shop I knew that the wind must be abating and time after time I knocked the snow from the windows and stood straining my eyes into that misty, vague out-of-doors. Ten o'clock, eleven o'clock. Something moved along the edge of the pond, the vague outlines of some animal, a slight lull in the wind and I could see that it was a horseman, another followed—I caught up a cape, flung open the door, dashed out into the storm through drifts, over every detaining obstacle until I reached the corral and—Owen.

They were safe, but so weary and worn they could scarcely speak. Their faces were swollen, having been whipped and lashed by the icy particles the wind had driven against them like bits of steel from a mighty blast furnace, their eyebrows and lashes were solid ice, their lips cracked and bleeding.

After a night of horror, at three in the morning, they had found Dorn at the Six Shooter camp comfortably sleeping with the Mexican herder! When the storm began he made no attempt to come back to the ranch, not stopping to think that his non-appearance would cause any anxiety, besides endangering the lives of two men.

"I was so hot when I seen Dorn nice and warm all cuddled up there with that Dago I jest drug him out by the collar and shook him. Anybody that'ud sleep with a Mexican had orter freeze to death. Gosh! Here was Mr. Brook and me amblin' over this whole blamed country, flounderin' through snow drifts as high as this house, gettin' our horses down and most freezin' to death, huntin' a no account thing like that." Bill was himself again.

Their knowledge of the country and presence of mind had saved them, for once when they found that it had grown warmer and apparently the wind had ceased, they realized that the horses had turned with the wind so that it was at their backs, they forced the poor things into the face of the bitter gale again and went on. They passed the camp without seeing it and had gone beyond when the wind brought them the smell of the sheep, they turned back and after searching found the cabin. It was a narrow escape for they were too exhausted to have gone farther.

A few days later we learned that old John, who had been our mail carrier, had perished in the storm. He had gone out to try to find his cattle and did not return. His wife and little son were alone and when they were able to get out and look for him, they found him just outside the garden fence lying frozen and half eaten by the coyotes.

I thought much during the following days and finally I came to a conclusion.

"Owen, if you want to sell out I'm willing— it will have to come some day, I realize that, and besides—there is too much at stake. I don't believe I can ever live through another blizzard."

In three months all the stock on the ranch

was sold, a caretaker was placed in charge of the home ranch, which we retained, and we moved to Denver. But instead of selling out to the syndicate, Owen decided to put our lands on the market himself and they were listed for sale.

It was the end of the old life; we had made way for the settlers.

XIII

ECHOES OF THE PAST

THE curtain of years had fallen and risen again on the same scene, the valley which stretched off toward the setting sun and the guardian mountain which stood unchanged at its head. But this was October, the royal season of purple and gold and red, when the asters and sunflowers were blooming their lives away in one lavish outpouring of beauty and the rose bushes were crimson under the kiss of the frost. A shimmering mass of gold clothed the great cotton-woods along the winding course of the creek and hills of russet brown replaced those of vivid green I had first seen sixteen years before.

Where the young bride had stood on that July day, amid the strange surroundings, looking with inexperienced eyes upon a new world, she stood again, seeing it from the angle of a participant, from the viewpoint of a woman, fused by the furnace of experience into a part of that life.

It was the same scene, but the setting had changed and as a flood of memories swept over me I felt as though I were a reincarnated spirit, walking the earth in a third phase of existence, having passed through the first, a light-hearted girl among family and friends in urban surroundings, having lived through the second, an atom in the midst of those vast wind-swept plains amongst elemental conditions, a part in the great primitive struggle for existence and coming back again to find the prairies transformed by cultivation into farms, with the crops covering the hills and bottom lands like a huge patch-work quilt of green, brown and brilliant yellow, fastened together with black threads of barbed wire.

Above on the hill stood a church and a school-house, those certain indications of community life. Across the meadows great red barns and towering wind mills overshadowed the less pretentious houses.

Bridges spanned the creek with its shifting, treacherous sand and in place of the dim winding trails across the prairie, neatly fenced county roads decorously followed the section lines.

It was the same—yet everything was changed. This well-ordered farming community seemed prosaic, it lacked the romance and charm of the old ranch life and the glorious sense of unlimited freedom.

The bunkhouse was occupied by the family of a hard-working farmer who had married the daughter of our caretaker, Parker; tractors, ploughs and harrows filled the space about the blacksmith shop. I resented those unfamiliar implements and the prosperous farms. On all sides there was heard a strange language of silos, separators and "crop rotation". I had become a part of the old life, but here I felt restricted and out of place—an alien.

Inside the house all, too, was changed. The books which Joe had scorned, the crystal clock and our Lares and Penates were in our Denver home, but on the ranch I missed them and most of all the old familiar faces. All had gone. Several of the boys had stayed in the country, married and taken up farming, raising bounteous crops and numerous children. Some, individual and picturesque to the end, had crossed the Great Divide, others had sought new positions in Wyoming, the last of the frontier states. Bill was there cooking in an oil camp. We received characteristic, though infrequent, letters from him, usually in the early summer, labored epistles over which he had "sworn and sweat," as he expressed it, which began by assuring us that he was well and hoped that we were the same and ended by an earnest request to go with us as cook "in case you was thinkin' of goin' campin'." He went with us when we did go, the same old Bill, unchanged in heart or humor.

Old Bohm was dead. The final act of that great tragedy took place in an isolated mine where he had sunk all his fortune in a golden prospect. Hoping to regain it, the fortune he held in trust for a friend had followed, but the game he had played so successfully before failed when Nemesis took a hand. His friend went to the mine to demand an accounting and several hours later Bohm's body, broken and bleeding, was taken from the depths of the mine. According to the story of his companion, the only witness, he had slipped and fallen to the bottom of the shaft—and his death, as his life, remained an enigma.

But down through the long years the echoes of the past reverberated. Again and again we heard them, sometimes very faintly, then with perfect distinctness and on that day of our return after a long absence we felt again that mysterious suggestion of tragedy and the echoes were startlingly clear.

As I came in from my walk just before supper, a strange man rode up and Mr. Parker asked him to stop.

He told us his name and during the progress of the meal took little part in the conversation, but after he had eaten his supper he leaned back in his chair and in response to Owen's question, said:

"No, I ain't exactly a stranger round here,

but this old kitchen is about the only thing that ain't changed. I used to know every inch of ground in this country when I was punchin' cows for the Three Circle outfit. This was the only ranch within twenty-five miles. I've et here lots of times."

"You knew the Bohms then?" I asked, trying as always to find the answer to the riddle of old Bohm's personality.

"Sure, I knew the Bohms," the stranger replied, his clear blue eyes meeting mine frankly. "I knowed everybody there was in the country, there wasn't many in them days, jest the Bohms, the Mortons, the Bosmans and the La Montes. They're most all gone now except Bosman. I heered old La Monte died last winter—but Lord, he's been worse 'en dead for most twenty years. Did you folks know him?"

"Scarcely, we only saw him once," and before me rose the picture of the desolate old place, the slowly opened door and that living ghost on the threshold.

The stranger again spoke.

"You folks bought from Bohm, so you knowed him, didn't you?"

"Oh, yes, we knew him." Owen answered for my thoughts were far away.

"Well, sir," said the old cow-puncher, reaching for a toothpick, "Jim Bohm was a great one, he was the slickest man in this country. He didn't have nothin' but a little band of horses that he drove up from Texas when he came, but he kept gettin' richer all the time." I came back to the present with a start, his words were almost the same Mrs. Morton had used sixteen years before.

"Wasn't he honest?" I asked, wondering what the reply would be.

He did not answer for a moment.

"Well, I can't say as to that. I jest knowed him from meetin' him on the round-ups and when I stopped here. I never had no dealin's with him, but he sure had a reputation for all the meanness there was, and I guess he deserved it. He was good company though, and Lord, how he could play the fiddle." He was interrupted by a sudden clatter. Mrs. Parker had dropped her spoon and was looking at him as if fascinated. "I liked Mrs. Bohm, but I never had no use for him. I don't know about the other things, but he

sure done Jean La Monte dirt." He rose
from the table and walked toward the door.
"Well, I reckon I'd better be movin' on, I
want to get to Bosman's tonight." He looked
up the valley, "I can see Bohm now, ridin'
that big black horse of his, carryin' a little
cotton-wood switch for a whip, and laughin'
at everything, he was a queer one, sure
enough. Well, so long—thank you for my
supper," and he went out into the evening.

"Big black horse! He was always on a
big black horse!" That pitiful refrain of
Jean La Monte as he had sought the rider
of that horse through all those weary years.
Again I saw the men waiting in the wagon
and that poor half-clad figure stooping to
pick up a little cotton-wood switch, and I
wondered if across the great divide LaMonte
had caught up with Bohm at last.

Owen was busy in the office making out
contracts for recently purchased land. Mr.
Parker and an agent were entertaining some
land-buyers, scraps of their conversation
"bushels to the acre" and "back in Kansas"

reached me from time to time as I walked up
and down under the stars.

"Where are you, childy?" Dear Mrs. Parker was always concerned when I was not in
sight. "Out there alone?" she asked as she
came across the yard to join me. We sat
down on the bunk-house steps, glorying in
the beauty of the night. We were silent for
a few moments and then she spoke.

"Do you know, Mrs. Brook, him talkin'
about Mr. Bohm tonight at supper has made
me think of so many things. I never paid
much attention to all them stories old Mrs.
Morton and other folks told, but some mighty
queer things have happened since we've been
here."

"What kind of things?" I asked, wondering
if she, too, had breathed the air of mystery
which surrounded the old ranch.

"Well, I don't know exactly," she hesitated,
"you'll think I'm silly, perhaps, but you know
sometimes when I'm down there," she pointed
to the house among the trees, "makin' out
my postal reports, sometimes it's eleven or
twelve o'clock before I'm through. It's awful

quiet after everyone's gone to sleep and I've heard all kinds of queer sounds, maybe they might be rats or the wind, but often and often, just as plain as I can hear your voice now, I've heard the sound of a violin like somebody was playin'. It give me an awful start when that man spoke of Bohm's havin' played the violin."

"Perhaps somebody is playing," I ventured, with a well remembered sensation of ice in the region of my spine. "The houses aren't far away now; you could easily hear someone playing if the wind was in the right direction."

Mrs. Parker shook her head.

"No, that ain't it. There ain't a violin in the country, and, besides, it's too near; it's like it came from here"—Mrs. Parker looked up at the bunkhouse door—"and none of Ethel's plays."

I said nothing. I remembered too well hearing the strains of the violin as they used to float out through the silent night while old Bohm played to himself up there in the bunkhouse, hour after hour. I was troubled as the echoes of the past grew louder.

"And then," Mrs. Parker resumed, "there was that passage. I told you about that, didn't I?"

"No. Passage! What passage?" I turned to her in the moonlight which showed a puzzled frown between her eyes.

"Why, the passage old Dad Patten found. I thought I'd told you about that, but maybe it was the year that you and Mr. Brook was away." She paused a moment. "The third year after Ethel and John came here, John, he raised such a big crop of potatoes the cellar was plumb full, so he had Dad tear out some of the old bins under the bunk house to make some larger ones. Tom Lane was helpin' him, and, of course, Tom was drunk. They'd tore out one or two, but when they come to the third, they found a deep hole behind it about four foot square. They stuck a spade into it, but it seemed to go back so far Dad he thought he'd investigate, so he begun to crawl into it to see how far it went. He was well in when Tom begun to laugh and act like he was goin' to wall him up, so Dad backed out, for he said that he was afraid Tom was just drunk enough to do it. Dad said, though, that he went in the whole length of his body and stretched his arm out as far as he could, but didn't touch nothin', so he knew it went on further, and he said that it seemed to lead off in the direction of the old root cellar."

"Root cellar," I repeated, too perturbed to say anything else.

"Yes," said Mrs. Parker, "but, you know, Dad, he'd never heard any of them stories about the root cellar; Dad's too deaf to hear anything, so he didn't think nothin' about it except that it was some kind of an old dugout, and they went on and built the new bins, and about two months after John had got all his potatoes in Dad happened to say something about it. I was so beat I like to died, and when I told Dad what folks said about the old root cellar and Bohm, he turned as white as a sheet. You couldn't get him up to the bunk house now if you was to drag him."

"You don't believe——" I began, then stopped as Mrs. Parker rose and put her hand on my shoulder.

"Childy, I don't know whether I believe

them tales or not. I've scarcely been off this place since you went away ten years ago and I've seen and heard some mighty strange things. There's lots of things in life we can't explain—we just have to accept 'em, and that's the way I've had to do here. Maybe there's spirits and maybe there ain't, but there's some facts there's no gettin' 'round"—Mrs. Morton's very words again—"but Dad's findin' that passage sure made me believe 'em more than I ever did before, and I do believe that some terrible things have been done right here on this dear old place, and that somewhere old Bohm's spirit's mighty restless."

Owen and I sat up before the fire talking until late that night, for one of the buyers wanted the home place. It was hard to give it up, for we both loved it, but the old life had passed, and we were not a part of the new. Owen's business kept him almost constantly in Denver, and we were at the ranch so little it seemed useless to cling to it longer. The most difficult decision had been made ten years before. This, in a way, was more simple, yet this was final; it meant the breaking of the last tie which bound us to those broad acres, and we were both silent a long time after we had agreed that it was best to let the old place go.

Suddenly I thought of my conversation with Mrs. Parker, and told Owen of the finding of the passage under the bunk house. He sat looking into the fire, and made no comment until I had finished.

"It is strange, to say the least. I don't suppose we shall ever know the real truth about it, but it doesn't make much difference now; and if old Bohm's spirit is wandering about here it will feel a little out of place in a cornfield."

"It certainly will, but, Owen, don't you hope 'it's mighty restless somewhere'?"

"Indeed I do," he laughed, and then grew serious again. "It's been wonderful from first to last, our life here." He sighed a little. "What experiences we've had!"

"Yes, it has," I said, getting up and standing by the fireplace, where Owen joined me. "It hasn't always been easy, but I wouldn't

take anything for the things I've learned.
I'm not the 'Tenderfoot' you brought out
sixteen years ago; I'm a dyed-in-the-wool
Westerner now. My whole view of life has
changed. It has not only been a wonderful
experience, Owen, but a wonderful privilege
—to have lived here."

Without a word we watched the last log
break apart. The glowing sparks lighted
the room for a single instant, then died
down, and in the fading light of the coals
we turned away.

That night I laid awake. Vivified by the
thought of the final parting which was to
come, our whole life on the ranch passed in
review before me, the problems and the
difficulties, the adjustments, the changed
conditions and that disturbing sense of un-
solved mystery.

I got up and stood by the window looking
out upon a world of silver. Myriads of
stars shone faintly in the heavens dimmed by
the glory of the moon, the pale outline of
the mountain was just visible, and, as on
that first day when my heart was so heavy,

I felt the sense of confusion give way to peace.

From the vast spaces, under the guardianship of that commanding summit, we had gained a new sense of proportion, freedom from hampering trivialities and a broader vision of life and its responsibilities.

Standing there in the moonlight facing the mountain, I saw in it more than a symbol and source of strength; to me it had become indeed the abiding place of a God.

Looking back over the years, all the changes revealed only the evolution of a wondrous plan. We had launched our frail barque in the midst of the prairie sea at the ebb of the tide of the wild, lawless days of the West; with the flow we had been carried through the years of a well-ordered pastoral existence to the era of agricultural productivity, and on each succeeding wave we had seen civilization borne higher and higher toward the ultimate goal set by the Great Spirit.

Ours had been, indeed, a wonderful experience.

THE END.